America!
You're Too Young To Die!

Chuck Anderson

xulon
PRESS

America! You're Too Young To Die!
by Chuck Anderson

Printed in the United States of America

ISBN 978-1-60266-156-1

All scripture references are from the King James Version, Scofield Reference Bible 1967 Edition by Oxford University Press.

Throughout the book, underlined portions of some quotations and some Biblical texts are made for emphasis by the author.

www.xulonpress.com

Published by:
GLOBAL OUTREACH MINISTRIES, INC.

America! You're Too Young To Die!

Charles S. Anderson

Table of Contents

Forward

Introduction

INTRODUCTION

The ruins of the ancient cities of Sodom and Gomorrah have been located along the western shores of the Dead Sea. They stand there in stark contrast to the mountains around them. God preserved the huge ruins of white ash as a reminder that God's Word, the Bible, is not a fairy tale to be taken lightly. His Word is literal and absolutely true.

Does the discovery of the cities destroyed by a torrential downpour of burning sulfur pellets have any implication for a modern, end-time nation that flaunts its immorality and perversion?

Will the tragic story of Sodom and Gomorrah ever be repeated?

The answer to these questions appears to be a tragic and resounding "yes." The ancient prophets of God spoke of a mighty, end-time nation that they referred to as *"the daughter of Babylon."* According to the prophets, the youngest and most powerful of all nations will one day experience the same tragic fate as Sodom and Gomorrah –

> *"As God overthrew Sodom and Gomorrah and their neighboring cities, saith the LORD, so shall no man abide there, neither shall any son of man dwell in her." Jeremiah 50:40*

After nearly 20 years of Biblical research, the author carefully reveals the Old Testament and New Testament descriptions of a great end-time nation that is referred to in the Scriptures as "Babylon" and the "daughter of Babylon." The reader will be surprised at the clarity with which the prophets wrote so long ago.

The warnings proclaimed clearly in God's Word, the Bible, should be taken seriously by all nations and individuals –

God *"turning the cities of Sodom and Gomorrah into ashes, condemned them with an overthrow, making them an example unto those that afterward should live ungodly . . ."* 2 Peter 2:6

In the midst of His message of coming doom upon an immoral, godless society, God also gives hope to those that will believe –

God *"delivered just Lot, vexed with the filthy manner of life of the wicked . . . The Lord knoweth how to deliver the godly out of temptations . . ."* 2 Peter 2:7, 9

"The Lord is not slack concerning His promise, as some men count slackness, but is longsuffering toward us, not willing that any should perish, but that all should come to repentance." 2 Peter 3:9

Chapter 1
"ASHES, ASHES,
WE ALL FALL DOWN"

I stood there stunned and in near disbelief as my feet sunk into the dry ash. I felt dazed and a little overwhelmed at what I was observing.

Here, near the foot of Masada on the western shores of the Dead Sea, lay the evidence of a once thriving city that was totally destroyed. The white ashen ruins are still preserved there for all the world to see and take heed.

The white ash was everywhere and in some areas it was so soft and deep that it made walking very difficult. To my amazement, I broke off a little piece of one of the ancient formations with my pocket knife and it just crumbled in my fingers. As I rubbed the crusted and flaky material between my fingers it turned into fine powder like white talcum. I wondered to myself, "What kind of inferno would it take to turn a city of solid stone into piles of white ash?"

The evidence that this was once a huge city was everywhere. Within the ruins one can see what appears to be rounded and square towers, archways, windows and doorways.

The most revealing view of the city was from the top of nearby Masada where you can get a true perspective of what a massive city this once had been. From this vantage point of over 1,000 feet above the city we could distinguish raised platform areas that were apparently temple sites with ziggurat-shaped and sphinx-shaped objects.

Scattered on the ground were golf ball sized pellets which I later discovered were 98% pure sulfur with small traces of magnesium. Sulfur found in its natural state is usually between 40 - 45% in purity along with other minerals. The high content of sulfur that I held in my hands would burn at an incredible temperature.

Tests performed by Wyatt Archeological Research revealed that the sulfur balls would burn at 482 degrees Fahrenheit (250 degrees Celsius). That's hot! Just like we read in the Bible, it had obviously *"rained fire and brimstone"* upon this ancient city. *"Brimstone"* in the text of *Genesis 19:24* is really the Hebrew word for "sulfur" – *"Then the LORD rained upon Sodom and upon Gomorrah BRIMSTONE* (sulfur) *and fire from the LORD out of heaven."*

FIERY CLOUDBURST!

In several areas, the sulfur pellets were easily visible all over the ground. Some were melted and still embedded into the limestone ash. It's hard to even imagine a literal cloudburst of burning sulfur. Nothing short of a blazing inferno could cause such total devastation.

My mind raced back to the many memories of hail storms I had experienced through the years. First a few white hailstones would bounce harmlessly on the ground and then, suddenly, an overwhelming torrent of heaven's fury would descend. It must have been similar to that on that fateful day when these cities were suddenly destroyed by a downpour of burning sulfur.

Handfuls of sulfur pellets can be found scattered all over the ground at the site of what is believed to be the ruins of Sodom and Gomorrah. Pictured above is George Gerak, one of the author's companions who visited the site in April, 2006.

Can you imagine the panic of the people? Some would try to take shelter in their homes, but the roofs would break out into a burning inferno. Each piece of this *"brimstone"* would be so hot that it would begin burning right into the solid limestone. The smoke and fumes would be immediately suffocating and overwhelming. And the burning rain apparently continued until the whole ground was covered and all the rock was thoroughly incinerated. What an incredible and terrible event that must have been! And once the firestorm began, there was no place to run . . . no place to hide! Only three people escaped.

Pictured above is what appears to be a man-made sphinx outside the ancient city of Gomorrah. Notice the obvious headband on the sphinx similar to the ones found in Egypt.

As you drive up the road approaching Masada, the mountain top fortress destroyed by the Romans in 73 A.D., there is a large dirt parking lot on the north side of the road. It is just a short walk going to the north-west where you can see what appears to be the ashen remains of the ancient sphinx.

It had probably been built there outside the main gate of the city to ward off enemies. The ancient pagans would erect idols and figures of their heathen gods by the main gates of their cities thinking they would somehow win their favor and be protected by them. Their idols had obviously failed them the day they met their burning doom. The sphinx still lays there in white ash just like the rest of the city as a sober reminder that God had judged this society for its sin and perversion.

There are several other interesting features you can observe as you enter what appears to be the main gate to the city. On the western edge of the large opening is a tall structure exactly like a gate "tower" typical of other Canaanite cities of the same era. You can also observe what appears to be a double outer wall to the city, typical of walls excavated at other ancient sites.

 Many of the ruins display 90 degree corners in contrast to natural formations where such obvious human workmanship is seldom found. The ruins also stand out in stark contrast

to the darker stone mountains in the background.

I had noticed the white ruins during my first trip to Israel in November, 2005, as I stood on top of Masada and as we traveled southward on the road along the Dead Sea, but from a distance I had not realized that they were the remnants of the infamous cities.

Soon after I returned home from that trip, I became fascinated with what archeological explorer Ron Wyatt had written about Sodom and Gomorrah. He had documented what he believed were the locations of Gomorrah and the other four "cities of the plain" during his work there in the 1980's. I had been right next to those sites and didn't even know it, so I returned to Israel to see them for myself in the spring of 2006.

After spending several hours collecting sulfur pellets, my three companions and I observed one high wall that still revealed the shadows of what appeared to be doors and windows, or possibly insets where idols might have been placed, similar to what can be observed at the ancient city of Petra. Gomorrah is an immense area and one could spend days just walking the site.

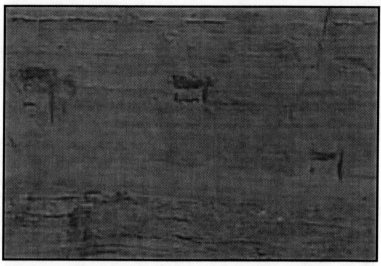

Shadows of what appears to be windows and doors at the ruins of Gomorrah near Masada.

Now I was standing there, in a place that had come under the awful judgment of God nearly 4,000 years ago. Imagine an entire city devastated by an all- consuming storm of burning sulfur!   I have to tell you that I was nearly overcome with emotion and sorrow that any civilization had become so decadent that God would wipe it off the face of the earth.

As we wandered around the ruins of Gomorrah, I wondered, **"Could this ever happen again to a modern society that lives the same carefree and immoral lifestyle?"**

NO FAIRY TALE
What we were observing were not the props of a mere fairy tale created from someone's wild imagination. This was

once a bustling city with thousands of residents. Now it was nothing more than eerie shapes and shadows apparently preserved by the One Who destroyed it.

The ancient Hebrew historian Josephus apparently visited the ruins in the first century. He spoke of the remains of these five cities destroyed by God –

> *"Now this country is then so sadly burnt up, that nobody cares to come at it; . . . It was of old a most happy land, both for the fruits it bore and the riches of its cities, although it be now all burnt up. It is related how for the impiety of its inhabitants, it was burnt by lightning; in consequence of which there are still the remainders of that divine fire; and the traces (or shadows) of the five cities are still to be seen . . . "(Josephus in his "Wars Of The Jews," book IV, chapter VIII)*

Shadows of the five cities are still to be seen . . ." wrote Josephus. Now, nothing remains but ashes and sulfur pellets!

A Tale of Five Cities

This site, which we believe is the ashen remains of ancient Gomorrah, is just north and east of the famous ruins of Masada. It is one of five cities located along the Dead Sea known as the *"cities of the plain"* and described in the Bible in *Genesis 13:12.*

From *Genesis 14:2* we learn that the names of the cities were Zeboim, Admah, Sodom, Gomorrah and Zoar. All five of the cities' ruins are the same white ash dotted by thousands of sulfur pellets. At the edge of each city the white ash abruptly ends. This was not a random act of nature!

DEAD SEA

Today, the entire area along the Dead Sea is little more than a desert wasteland. The Dead Sea is 1350 feet below sea level – the lowest point on earth. The water is now so contaminated with minerals and salt, that it is the consistency of 10 weight motor oil.

The Dead Sea is one of the richest spots on earth, and both Israel and Jordan are mining the minerals at the extreme southern end. But the Dead Sea is virtually dead. Nothing lives in its waters. In my opinion, the entire Dead Sea region bears the marks of an area that came under the severe judgment and curse of God. Even the surrounding hills are bleak and lifeless.

". . . well watered everywhere"!

The Dead Sea Valley which is called the Arabah, has not always been a desert wasteland. Lot, the nephew of Abraham, was attracted to the area – *"And Lot lifted up*

his eyes, and beheld all the plain of Jordan, that <u>it was well</u>
<u>watered everywhere</u>, before the LORD destroyed Sodom and
Gomorrah, <u>even as the garden of the LORD</u>, like the
land of Egypt, as thou comest unto Zoar. Then Lot chose
him all the plain of Jordan; and Lot journeyed east . . . and
Lot pitched his tent toward Sodom . . ." Genesis 13:10-12

Before the LORD destroyed the cities, the entire valley was
like a garden -- the Bible says *"as the garden of the*
LORD." Many believe that before the cities were
decimated, the Dead Sea itself was alive, teeming with fish
and wildlife. According to the Biblical record, grass and
wild life were found in great abundance. Little wonder that
numerous cities would be developed along the shores of the
sea.

Later, the descendents of Lot would build other cities along
the eastern shore of the sea and their ruins are still visible
today, destroyed not by a deluge of fire but by warfare.
Huge cemeteries are also visible along the eastern shore of
the Dead Sea on the Jordanian side, attesting to the fact that
the Moabites lived along the sea in great numbers.

Through the years, the Dead Sea has apparently become
saltier and saltier because of evaporation and decreased
water flow. Most of the water that once flowed into the
Dead Sea from the Jordan River is now being used by both
Israel and Jordan to irrigate the fertile farm lands that run
just north of the Dead Sea up to the Sea of Galilee.

You can be sure that no thriving community in need of fresh
water is being built along its shores today!   One wonders if

the pre-judgment sea had an underground water channel so the waters would remain fresh and clear. There are many places on earth where rivers simply disappear underground. Fresh water flowing through the sea would have made it a most pleasant lake instead of the stagnant leach pond it is today.

A peninsula still extends out into the Dead Sea from the ruins of Gomorrah right near the foot of Masada. It, too, must have been inhabited, because it also bears the evidence of destruction by fire. The same ash and a few sulfur pellets have been found there.

Gomorrah may have once been a beautiful sea resort with wonderful beaches and fresh water. One can imagine that the cities of the plain were once busy communities with open-air markets, restaurants and happy voices. Something obviously attracted Lot and his family to live there!

GRIM REMINDER
God has left those ruins there for all to see as an example and warning for all generations –

God *"turned the cities of Sodom and Gomorrah into ashes . . . making them an example unto those that afterward should live ungodly." 2 Peter 2:6*

This warning is so important that God repeated the message in *Jude, verse 7* – *"Even as Sodom and Gomorrah, and the cities about them in going after strange flesh, are set forth for an example suffering the vengeance of eternal fire."*

Fire and sulfur literally rained upon Sodom and Gomorrah!

My heart was especially heavy as I walked around the white ashes of Gomorrah, because I knew that I was previewing the terrible destruction that is prophesied to happen again to another end-time society. Jeremiah foretold the utter destruction of a future nation that he referred to as *"the daughter of Babylon"*-

> *"As God overthrew Sodom and Gomorrah and their neighboring cities, saith the LORD, so shall no man abide there, neither shall any son of man dwell in her."* *Jeremiah 50:40*

FUTURE DEVASTATION

The impact of the future destruction of "Babylon" will be so great that the entire planet will be affected – *"At the noise of the taking of Babylon <u>the earth is moved</u>, and the cry is* *heard among the nations."*

The weapons that the LORD calls against Babylon will be so powerful that the earth will literally be moved out of orbit. Can you imagine such destructive fury? *Isaiah 13:13* adds to this terrible image of carnage, *"I will shake the heavens, and <u>the earth shall remove out of its place</u>, in the wrath of the LORD of hosts, and in the day of His fierce anger."*

A WARNING FOR FUTURE GENERATIONS
The end-time *"daughter of Babylon,"* slated for destruction, is described by Jeremiah as a powerful and wealthy nation, the youngest of all the great nations and a country that is born from a motherland. This is obviously not referring to the ancient Babylonian Empire which is the oldest of the nations.

Jeremiah wasn't the only prophet to speak of a future day of calamity upon the end-time nation called Babylon. Isaiah presented the same warning almost word for word -- *"And Babylon, the glory of kingdoms, the beauty of the Chaldeans' excellency, shall be as when God overthrew Sodom and Gomorrah. It shall never be inhabited, neither shall it be dwelt in from generation to generation . . ."* *Isaiah 13:19*

This particular prophecy could have overtones to the future destruction of the historical site of Babylon south of Baghdad because the prophet specifically mentions *"the Chaldeans' excellency,"* but the bigger picture of the multitude of prophecies against Babylon refers to a huge end-time nation that is the world center of political influence and economic commerce.

It is interesting to note that ancient Babylon was never destroyed by fire. After the death of Alexander the Great the city was abandoned, and through the centuries it slowly crumbled and faded away. The once glorious city of Nebuchadnezzar's empire became the dwelling place of Bedouins. Ancient Babylon never experienced the fiery wrath of God as described by the prophets.

SADDAM'S ROYAL CITY?

Some believe that all of the prophecies were directed toward the rebuilt city of Babylon. They believe that the effort begun by Saddam Hussein will one day become the greatest city on earth. I personally doubt that the most powerful nation on earth will rise up from the desert ruins of ancient Babylon.

Rebuilt Palace at Saddam's Babylon.

Indeed, the buildings and ruins of Saddam's Babylon may one day be destroyed by fire, but the prophecies were, without doubt, directed toward a different and thriving nation – Babylon's *"daughter."* These end-time prophecies have not yet been fulfilled.

Some day in the future, perhaps sooner than we care to imagine, a large, wealthy and thriving end-time society will be turned into burning rubble and ashes just as the prophets foretold. That day of destruction will be equal to the terrible judgment of Sodom and Gomorrah. Should not our hearts break over the tragic prophecy of coming doom? In a later chapter we will consider the many descriptions and possible identity of that end-time nation facing judgment.

GOD WILL NOT TOLERATE SIN AND PERVERSION FOREVER

There is a solemn lesson to learn as you come to grips with God's outpoured fury against Sodom and Gomorrah -- God will not tolerate immorality and perversion forever.

Why Lot and his family chose to live in Sodom is beyond our imagination, because the Bible tells us that *"the men of Sodom were wicked and sinners before the LORD exceedingly." Genesis 13:13*

What was Lot, a believer in the LORD, doing in such a place? Perhaps the answer to why Lot would take his entire household into such a community is revealed in *Ezekiel 16:49-50 – "Behold, this was the iniquity of thy sister Sodom, pride, fullness of bread, and abundance of Idleness was in her and in her daughters, neither did she strengthen the hand of the poor and the needy. And they were haughty, and committed abomination before Me; therefore I took them away as I saw good."*

This was a wealthy and successful community. Food and anything one could imagine were probably available in great abundance. There was plenty of leisure time and no shortage of entertainment. Apparently the cities offered many attractive features to Lot and his family and they were happy to abandon the hardships of living in tents in the wilderness.

Moses warned the people of Israel that easy living and material wealth had their pitfalls – *"It shall be, when the LORD thy God shall have brought thee into the land which He swore unto thy fathers, to Abraham, to Isaac, and to Jacob, to give thee great and goodly cities, which thou buildedst not, And houses full of all good things, which thou filledst not, and wells digged, which thou diggedst not, vineyards and olive trees, which thou plantedst not, when thou shalt have eaten and be full; Then beware lest thou forget the LORD, Who brought thee forth out of the land of Egypt, from the house of bondage." Deuteronomy 6:10-12*

Isn't it sad that an abundance of leisure and possessions often leads to great sin and immorality? What a great tragedy that Lot would subject his family to all the luxuries, evil influence, and eventual destruction of a degenerate and wicked society! Lot had many herdsmen and servants, in addition to his immediate family, and they all perished in the cities of the plain except for Lot himself and two daughters.

Four thousand years later we need to take heed lest our great abundance becomes a stumbling stone for us and the ones we love.

I fear that the sinful ways of our modern world have become so commonplace and acceptable that we have all become hardened and calloused to the very things that God deplores. Nothing is shocking to us anymore, and sin and perversion have become an ever increasing part of the world in which we live.

A MODERN DAY SODOM
Not only does modern society condone open immorality and perversion, but the aggressive agenda of ungodly activists is to purge public life of any remembrance of God and to thrust their immoral and evil lifestyle upon every part of society. Their deviate goal is to permeate all segments of our world and reach out with wicked fingers to every unsuspecting and unprotected child. May God forgive us and help us!

God's grace and mercy will someday be stretched beyond the limit. The prophets of old warned that there would be an end-time nation that would face the awful judgment of God.

LESSONS FROM THE PAST!
It has been wisely observed – "If we do not learn from history we are destined to repeat it!"

TWO BIG QUESTIONS:

#1 <u>WHO</u> is this unnamed nation described as the *"daughter of Babylon"* that will be destroyed like Sodom and Gomorrah?

#2 Is there any indication in the Scriptures <u>WHEN</u> this day of fiery judgment will occur?

Sulfur pellets scattered on the ground!

Ruins of man-made structures at Gomorrah.

Chapter 2
WHICH BABYLON?

The pronouncements of coming judgment upon the end-time *"daughter of Babylon"* should capture our full attention, or at least our curiosity. **Who is this** ***"Babylon"*** **described by the prophets and destined to become like Sodom and Gomorrah?** Actually, there are several different *"Babylons"* identified throughout the Scriptures.

ANCIENT RELIGIOUS BABYLON

The first "Babylon," of course, is the oldest, which I refer to as *"ancient religious Babylon."* The original city was established by Nimrod and was characterized by the *"tower whose top may reach heaven."* This ancient society can be found on the pages of Scripture in *Genesis, chapter 11.*

The ruins of ancient Babylon reveal that it was a highly developed civilization. By 2900 B.C. they had invented the wheel, dug canals from the Euphrates River in order to irrigate their crops, and had already established the sixty-minute hour plus the 360 degree circle.

Relics found at the site of the Tower of Babel reveal that they had made many remarkable advancements including a written language and advanced studies in mathematics. Of course, they were into astrology; thus the probable reason for erecting the high temple tower called a ziggurat. According to World Book Encyclopedia, the ancient Babylonians were even able to predict eclipses in the sun and moon. These people were not cavemen by any stretch of the imagination!

Speculation abounds as to why God confused the people by sending forth many languages. *Genesis 10:6* reveals – *"And the LORD God said, Behold, the people are one, and they have all one language; and this they begin to do; and now nothing will be withheld from them, which they have imagined to do."*

It was once observed – "Whatever man can conceive in his mind, he will someday be able to achieve." Is it possible that whatever man can imagine is technically possible? Perhaps so.

It is interesting to observe that the majority of all modern day inventions have taken place during the past century. Up until the early 1900's, man was limited to horse-drawn carts for travel and wood-burning fires for heat and cooking. It had been that way since the dawn of human history.

Now, suddenly, during the past 100 years knowledge has literally exploded, and we have made amazing technological advancements. In fact, man has developed so much that he now has the ability to destroy himself and the entire earth he lives in with weapons of unimaginable power.

Had man continued as he was going during the days of ancient Babylon, he might have attained the same destructive power long ago. Perhaps God, in His mercy and wisdom, confused the languages in order to keep man alive long enough to send a Redeemer and Savior.

It is especially noteworthy that the pagan religion of the ancient Babylonians has permeated nearly every religion on earth. After Nimrod's death, his wife, Semiramis, gave birth to a child that she named Tammuz. She claimed that his birth was by a miraculous conception by the sun god and that the baby was the reincarnation of Nimrod. Soon people began to worship her and her infant son, and she became the symbol of fertility and the "queen of all heaven."

The ongoing influence of the worship of Nimrod's wife and her "miracle" baby has impacted most of the world's religions, and many still worship the *"queen of heaven"* in one form or another even to this day.

Chinese Shingmoo and son

The Greeks also worshipped the goddess Aphrodite who was shown with child in arms.

Many of the pagan idols were considered the *"queen mother of heaven."*

India's goddess Indrani and son

Artemas: Greek goddess

The Egyptian goddess Isis and son

Even the Egyptians worshipped the man-made goddess of heaven and her son. Their idol was called Isis. The Hebrews were well aware of this pagan worship since they were slaves in the land of the pharaohs for 400 years. Later, the Romans also became involved with the same demonic religion and worshipped Venus and her male child, Jupiter. The list goes on and on. At the pagan city of Ephesus, the first-century preacher, Paul, encountered the same worship when he confronted the people who worshipped the goddess Diana. A great temple had been erected for her in Ephesus, and the people considered her the *"queen of heaven."*

Finally, the false goddess worship which began at the Tower of Babel infected the Christian church. After winning a great battle against his enemies under the sign of the cross, Roman Emperor Constantine the Great declared "Christianity" as the official religion of Rome. He "baptized" his Roman legions by marching

them through a river. Of course, the pagan masses brought their idolatrous worship into the church with them, and it was only a matter of time before the bishops met at the Counsel of Ephesus in A.D. 431 and approved the worship of the Virgin Mary as official church dogma. That practice thrives in the Roman church to this day.

Regardless of the name, the worship of the *"queen of heaven"* began at Babylon as Satan's great counterfeit and mockery of the virgin birth of the Lord Jesus Christ.

It is surprising that even the ancient people of Israel became entangled in this ungodly practice of goddess and baby worship. When confronted with their sin of idolatry, the people rejected Jeremiah's message to repent – *"As for the word that thou hast spoken unto us in the Name of the LORD, we will not hearken unto thee. But we will certainly do whatsoever thing goeth forth out of our own mouth, <u>to burn incense unto the queen of heaven</u>, and to pour out drink offerings unto her, as we have done, we, and our fathers, our kings, and our princes, in the cities of Judah, and in the streets of Jerusalem; for then had we plenty of food, and were well, and saw no evil." Jeremiah 44:16-17*

This was God's covenant people, the children of Israel, worshipping a pagan goddess at the Temple in Jerusalem!

Furthermore, the women of Judah gathered at a standing idol erected by the Temple in Jerusalem and prayed the most heathen of prayers – *"Then he brought me to the door of the gate of the LORD's house, which was toward the north; and, behold, there sat women weeping for Tammuz." Ezekiel 8:14* Some believe that these deceived women were praying that they would be instrumental in giving birth to yet another reincarnation of Nimrod. Perhaps they were praying that their messiah would be born supernaturally through them.

STANDING IDOLS
A common practice among many of the ancient civilizations was to erect a *"standing idol,"* also known as the *"ashteroth,"* in front of their pagan temple

or on high places throughout the countryside. These disgusting symbols were called phalli, and were stone images of the male sex organ. They have been found by the thousands all over the world. The degenerative pagans worshipped these idols that represented the heathen fertility gods.

Later cultures became "refined" and changed the vile appearance of the phallus to the more acceptable obelisk.

Of special interest is the fact that one of two identical obelisks that originated in Heliopolis, Egypt, has the inscription – *"I, Dionysus, dedicated these phalli to Hera, my stepmother."* The other obelisk was taken to Rome by Emperor Caligula where it was erected on a hill called his "circus." This is the hill where the Vatican was later built. In 1586 Pope Sixtus V had it moved to the front of the church at St. Peter's Square where it still stands to this day.

"Standing Idol" at St. Peter's Square in Rome

The symbol of the fertility cult of Nimrod has been associated with Baal worship and with the temple of Diana in Ephesus. The symbol of the phallus is even apparent at Mecca, the most sacred site of Islam, and at mosques throughout the world. Most people have no idea that the symbolism originated in ancient Babylon and was associated with the pagan fertility gods.

"Standing Idols" in Mecca

The largest obelisk in the world is located right here in the United States of America. The impressive five-hundred-fifty-five foot high Washington Monument is displayed in front of our national capital in Washington D.C. Some people are convinced that the significance of America's national obelisk is that it, too, represented the heathen fertility gods, and that in the minds of the designers it was an appropriate symbol in paying tribute to the "father" of our nation. This is very unfortunate, especially in light of the fact that the aluminum top cap displays the words "Laus Deo" which means "Praise Be To God."

In all fairness, it should be noted that the obelisk in Washington D.C. does not represent anything having to do with ancient paganism in the minds of most people. Placed within the cornerstone of the monument laid on July 4, 1848, is a Holy Bible, presented by the American Bible Society, and other items that attest to our dependence upon God and to our national motto, "One Nation Under God."

To most of us living today, the Washington Monument has absolutely nothing to do with the detestable idols of the pagan world, but we should at least be aware of where the symbols originated and what they represented in days gone by.

According to *"The Two Babylons"* by Hislop, these obelisks, or standing images, are mentioned in the Old Testament as part of Baal worship. Baal is one of the names for Nimrod. This was the false religion that Jezebel brought into ancient Israel along with all of its immoral practices. This heathen practice of idolatry and goddess worship is still alive and well today.

Dr. Noah Hutchings, founder of Southwest Radio Church, has done a monumental work on the research of Nimrod's ancient religion. He has dedicated a good portion of his books, *"Petra"* and *"U.S. in Prophecy,"* to that study. Much of the material used here was gleaned from his writings, and this author, for one, appreciates Dr. Hutchings' many years of faithful research and ministry of Biblical truth.

HISTORIC BABYLON

Historic Babylon was the first great world empire which came to the zenith of its power under the leadership of King Nebuchadnezzar. After the destruction of Jerusalem in 586 B.C., Daniel and a number of other young promising Jews were taken to the city of Babylon. It was there that God allowed Daniel to greatly prosper in the King's palace, and God gave him many wonderful opportunities to be a spokesman and witness of the greatness of the one true God, Jehovah.

King Nebuchadnezzar had a troubling dream of a huge statue whose head was pure gold, the arms and chest were

silver, the belly was brass, the legs were iron, and the feet were part iron, part clay. Daniel interpreted the dream for the king, and he revealed the sequence of all the future Gentile world kingdoms.

Daniel declared that Nebuchadnezzar and his Babylonian Empire were symbolized by the head of gold. His empire would give way to the divided and inferior empires of the Medes and Persians (arms and chest of silver). The third world empire would be that of Alexander the Great as he would lead his Greek army to world conquest. Then, of course, would come the Roman Empire, and, finally, the revived Roman Empire depicted by the ten toes made of iron and clay.

With remarkable accuracy, the predictions of Daniel have all come to pass with the exception of the revived Roman Empire. It will be the kingdom of the anti-Christ and his reign of terror during the future seven years of Tribulation. One day, perhaps very soon, the Roman Empire will be revived under the satanically empowered leadership of a false messiah who will deceive Israel and the peoples of the world by promising them universal peace. For a short time he will make good on his promise and will apparently allow them to rebuild the Third Temple in Jerusalem. Then, after the Temple is complete, suddenly his true character will be revealed and his reign of terror will begin.

Cloak and Dagger
The anti-Christ as described in *Daniel chapters 8 and 11* and *Revelation chapter 13*, will instigate a horrendous blood bath against the people of Israel and all peoples of faith, three and one-half years after he has confirmed a covenant with the Jews and promises them protection and peace – *"And he shall confirm the covenant with many for one week; and in the midst of the week, he shall cause the sacrifice and the oblation to cease, and for the overspreading of abominations he shall make it desolate, even until the consummation, and that determined shall be poured upon the desolate." Daniel 9:27*

Jesus spoke of the abomination to be committed by the man of sin in *Matthew 24:15-16* – *"When ye, therefore, shall see the abomination of desolation, spoken of by Daniel the prophet, stand in the holy place (whosoever readeth, let him understand), Then let them who are in Judea flee into the mountains . . ."*

It should be noted that, according to the Scriptures, the Temple sacrifices will once again be practiced. Thus, we know that one day the Temple will be rebuilt. This will occur under the deception of the wicked world leader who will enter the Temple and demand to be worshipped.

Just As The Prophets Said
As predicted by Daniel, all of the world kingdoms have come and gone, and the world now awaits the final chapter of Gentile world rule under the revived Roman Empire and the tyranny of the anti-Christ.

Historically, as prophesied, the ancient Babylonian Empire was given to the Medes and Persians as they quickly took the city without bloodshed and then killed King Belshazzar. The point is, historic Babylon was never destroyed by fire and turned to ash like Sodom and Gomorrah, as was prophesied in *Isaiah 13:19* – *"And Babylon, the glory of kingdoms, the beauty of the Chaldeans' excellency, shall be as when God overthrew Sodom and Gomorrah."* The prophecies given about the destruction of Babylon remain prophetic and are events yet to be fulfilled.

SADDAM'S REBUILT BABYLON
Some Bible students believe that all of the prophecies have

either been fulfilled or are related to the destruction of a rebuilt Babylon. There has been a modern rebuilding effort that has taken place in recent years at the historical site of Babylon located in Iraq 50 miles south of Baghdad. The reconstruction efforts of Saddam Hussein, the infamous "Butcher of Baghdad," may be destroyed in the future, but this will be just a partial fulfillment of the many prophesies against Babylon.

Saddam's Rebuilt Royal Palace in the new Babylon

Saddam made quite an impressive attempt to rebuild the famous city of Babylon, but the restored city is anything but a great economic and military power that impacts the rest of the world, as described in the Scriptures. With the fall of Saddam and his tyrannical government, it is uncertain what the future of the ancient city will be, but it is doubtful that it will ever equal the splendor or power of the city under ancient King Nebuchadnezzar.

The deposed leader of Iraq may have thought he was the reincarnation of the ancient King Nebuchadnezzar, but his attempts to restore the glory of the ancient city of Babylon have been meager, at best. The Prophets obviously had something else in mind when they predicted that *"the daughter of Babylon"*  would become like the destroyed cities of Sodom and Gomorrah and the world would weep *"for no man buyeth their merchandise any more . . ." Revelation 18:11*

END-TIME, RELIGIOUS BABYLON

Revelation, chapter 17 deals with end-time religious Babylon which will permeate religious thought during the times when the false messiah, anti-Christ, will come to power. Attempts will be made to bring the world under a "New World Order" of religious unity. It is interesting that this end-time religious system is called *"Mystery Babylon the Great, the <u>mother of harlots</u> and abominations of the earth." Revelation 17:5*

A study of the *seventeenth chapter of Revelation* reveals that this powerful religious system will be beautiful in the eyes of the world but is a harlot; that is, she will sell the truth for political power and her "lovers" are the kings of the world. The final verse in the chapter declares, *"And the woman* *whom thou sawest is that great city, which <u>reigneth over the kings of the earth.</u>"*

This great city of religious Babylon will be built on seven hills and shall apparently be burned with fire as we read in *verse 16 – "And the ten horns (ten kings) which thou sawest upon the beast, these shall hate the harlot, and shall make her desolate and naked, and shall eat her flesh, and <u>burn her with fire.</u>"*

Many believe that the religious *"harlot"* may refer to the Vatican with all of its pageantry and idolatry. Whoever *"Mystery Babylon the Great, the Mother of Harlots"* is, it will eventually be destroyed by the anti-Christ, or *"man of sin,"* as he declares himself to be "god" and demands worship.

END-TIME POLITICAL BABYLON

There are so many vivid descriptions of *"the daughter of Babylon"* that we will devote the entire next chapter to the subject and lay out each description point by point as they are presented in the Scriptures.

When I began this research many years ago, I was unaware that Dr. Franklin Logsdon wrote on the subject. Dr. Logsdon was the pastor of the famed Moody Church in Chicago, and his book, "Is The U.S. A. in Prophecy?" was published in 1968 by Zondervan Publishing Company. His work has now been reprinted with additional comments by Dr. Noah Hutchings.

Dr. Logsdon probably discovered, as I have, that revealing unpleasant things that appear to be pointed to our own beloved country is not well received. However, I feel that to be true to one's convictions is more important than the approval of man.

The words of Ezekiel have prompted me to finally make my own findings known:

"Son of man, I have made thee a watchman unto the house of Israel; therefore, hear the word at my mouth and give them warning from Me. When I say unto the wicked, Thou shalt surely die; and thou givest him not warning, nor speakest to warn the wicked from his wicked way, to save his life, the same wicked man shall die in his iniquity; but his blood will I require at thine hand." Ezekiel 3:17-18

Chapter 3
THE DESCRIPTION OF
"THE DAUGHTER OF BABYLON"

God does not speak with idle and wasteful words. He is not grasping for something to say just to fill the pages of a book. His words are not random thoughts to be ignored. We may not understand every word spoken, but I can assure you that every word from God is significant and has an eternal purpose.

There are more prophecies written in the Bible about an end-time nation called *"Babylon"* than about any other nation with the exception of Israel.

IGNORED PROPHECIES
It amazes me how few men have even attempted to understand the significance of the prophecies related to the *"daughter of Babylon."* God gave us His Word to provide light for a darkened world, and faithful students should seek a full knowledge of all portions of Scripture.

Because of the vast number of references that paint a vivid portrait of Babylon, I will deal with each of the major passages very <u>briefly</u> and present the descriptions in the order in which they are given in the Biblical text. I will also number them for ease of reference. Any repeated descriptions from other passages will be numbered to reference them back to the first description.

Jeremiah Chapter 50

The entire chapter of Jeremiah 50 is given to the study of Babylon. The LORD begins by declaring – _"The Word that the LORD spoke against Babylon."_ What a sobering and over-whelming statement that is. What message could possibly be worse, _"The Word that the LORD spoke against Babylon?"_

God, by His very nature, is the Lord of love, forgiveness and grace. _2 Peter 3:9_ says – _"The Lord is not slack concerning His promise . . . but is longsuffering toward us, NOT WILLING THAT ANY SHOULD PERISH, but that all should come to repentance."_

The statement that the LORD is _"against"_ Babylon is an indication that they will have apparently pushed the limit of His patience and grace. They may have had ample opportunities to turn to Him in repentance, but rejected His pleas.

The God who extended His mercy to a godless society like ancient Nineveh invites all men and nations to turn to Him and live. But woe to any nation that has had the Word of God and has carelessly spurned it! God's mercy eventually comes to an end.

1.   LATTER DAYS
Babylon is described as a nation that exists during the time that the people of Israel are returning to their land. _"In those days, and in that time, saith the LORD, the children of Israel shall come, they and the children of Judah together,_

going and weeping; they shall go, and seek the LORD, their God." (verse 4)

What an incredible time to be living! We are witnessing the return of God's chosen nation to their land. Jewish immigrants from all over the world are returning to the land of their promised dreams. However, most of them are not yet returning in repentance and faith in their Messiah. Like the valley full of dry bones *(Ezekiel chapter 37)* they have begun coming together, bone to bone, but as a nation, there is no spiritual breath in them – *". . . there was a noise and behold, a shaking, and the bones came together, bone to its bone. And when I beheld, lo, the sinews and the flesh came up upon them, and the skin covered them above, but there was no breath in them." Ezekiel, 37:7-8*

Genuine, born-again believers who have placed their faith in the Lord Jesus Christ rejoice at seeing the prosperity of the people of Israel. They are once again coming into their land, and we rejoice with them. But God's greatest work, turning the hearts of the nation toward Him and re-gathering them in mass, is yet future. Scripture tells us that someday the nation of Israel will recognize their Messiah whom they have rejected and millions will return to the land of their forefathers –

"A new heart also will I give you, and a new spirit will I put within you; and I will take away the stony heart out of your flesh, and I will give you an heart of flesh. And I will put my Spirit within you, and cause you to walk in my statutes, and ye shall keep mine ordinances, and do them. And ye shall dwell in the land that I gave to your

fathers; and ye shall be my people, and I will be your God." Ezekiel 36:26-28

Ezekiel recorded another great promise to the nation of Israel – *"And ye shall know that I am the LORD, when I have opened your graves, O my people, and brought you up out of your graves* (the gentile nations), *And shall put my Spirit in you, and ye shall live, and I shall place you in your own land; then shall ye know that I, the LORD, have spoken it." Ezekiel 37:13-14*

What a wonderful day of renewal and blessing is coming upon God's chosen nation – *"A new heart also will I give you, and a new spirit will I put within you; and I will take away the stony heart out of your flesh, and I will give you an heart of flesh." Ezekiel 36:26*

It is during these last days when the people of Israel are once again beginning to return to their land, that the *"the daughter of Babylon"* will exist.

2.   FLEE!
The people of Israel will flee out of Babylon – *"Flee out of the midst of Babylon, and go forth out of the land . . ." (verse 8)* The day is coming when thousands, perhaps even millions of people will panic and evacuate their homes and seek a place of safety and refuge. The fact that they will flee from everything they have known and loved paints a pathetic picture of calamity that is destined upon the end-time *"daughter of Babylon."*

Such panic that would create this kind of mass exodus from

a modern day nation is beyond our comprehension.

Jeremiah 51:46 may offer us a clue why there would be such a fearful evacuation – *"And lest your heart faint, and ye fear for the <u>rumor</u> that shall be heard in the land; a <u>rumor</u> shall both come one year, and after that in another year shall come a <u>rumor</u>, and violence in the land . . ."*

What kind of rumor would cause such mass hysteria that people would flee their homes and seek refuge in their ancestral homelands? Will it be fear of weapons of mass destruction in the hands of madmen and terrorists? Time will tell.

3.   A SAFE HAVEN FOR JEWS

There is another important description to observe in the preceding verse *(Jeremiah 50:8)* as God warns His people – *"<u>Flee out of the midst of Babylon.</u>"* This statement would imply that the people of Israel will be dwelling in end-time Babylon, and God tells them to run.

America! A safe-haven for the people of Israel.

This cannot possibly be referring to modern day Iraq where efforts have been made to revive the historic city of Babylon by Saddam Hussein. Iraq is far from being a safe refuge for Jews. End-time Babylon will obviously be a safe haven for Jews, and God warns His people to flee to their homeland before the fires of judgment fall.

4.   BORN FROM A MOTHERLAND

End-time Babylon will be born from a motherland – *"Your mother shall be completely confounded, she that bore you shall be ashamed." Jeremiah 50:12* This passage cannot possibly refer to the oldest of nations which was historical Babylon. How many nations can we name that claim they were "born" from a "motherland?" America is certainly one of very few. Two hundred years after the founding of our nation, it is still recognized by all that England is America's motherland.

Babylon's motherland is even described by the prophets.

5.   A SHRIVELED UP MOTHER
Referring to the *"mother of Babylon,"* the LORD uses very interesting language in describing her.   According to Jeremiah, she will become *"completely confounded."*

The Hebrew word for confounded means "completely dried up or pale." The word describes one who has shriveled up and lost all strength.

What an apt description of modern day England.   On January 16, 1968, the United Press International released an article under the caption of *"The Nightfall Of An Empire."* The article states, *"Britain yesterday abandoned her role as a world power.   British Prime minister Wilson's announcement before the House of Commons came after more than thirty-one hours of agonizing soul-searching by the British Cabinet."*

There was a time when Brits proudly claimed that the sun never set on their empire. Those days are gone forever, and the British world-wide empire has literally vanished. The *"mother of Babylon"* is truly confounded, or all shriveled up. What a remarkable prophetic utterance from a prophet that lived 2500 years before the fulfillment.

6.   A SHAMEFUL MOTHERLAND
The "mother" of end-time Babylon will be ashamed – *"Your mother shall be completely confounded, she that bore you*

shall be ashamed." (verse 12) One wonders what would cause such shame: Will the "mother" of end-time Babylon forsake her "daughter" in the hour of her greatest need? Will England abandon her "child" in time of future conflict?

As I write, Great Britain is one of the only faithful allies to the American effort against terrorism. Her allegiance, however, could change very quickly, especially if terrorists ignite a weapon of mass destruction in either of these countries. The fact is, the strength of the entire NATO alliance has greatly diminished since the end of the "cold war." America could very well find itself totally alone if the present conflict with terrorism accelerates and weapons of mass destruction are deployed or if British Prime Minister Tony Blair resigns his leadership.

7. THE YOUNGEST OF NATIONS

End-time Babylon will be clearly identified as the youngest of the great nations – *"behold the hindermost of the nations" (verse 12).* Hindermost means last, or youngest. Whoever this great nation is, it will be one that is relatively young compared to the ancient nations. With little more than two hundred years to our history, the United States of America is recognized as a mere "teenager" in comparison to the older nations of the world.

8. SINFUL NATION

End-time Babylon – *". . . hath sinned against the LORD." (verse 14)* What nation has NOT sinned against the holiness of God? But this nation, the *"daughter of Babylon,"* is destined to judgment and total ruin because of some sin that God deplores.

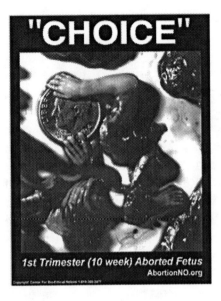

"CHOICE"

1st Trimester (10 week) Aborted Fetus
AbortionNO.org

What sin could possibly be so grave as to trigger the destructive wrath of the Righteous, Holy and Just God?

Could it be the thrusting of His Name out of all public life, or the acceptance of evil and perversion? Could it be the terrible slaughter of the innocent as performed at so-called "women's health clinics?" Whatever it is, God is not pleased with end-time Babylon, and judgment WILL someday fall!

There is a very revealing text in the Bible that details the downward spiral that caused God to destroy ancient Sodom –

> *"Behold, this is the iniquity of thy sister Sodom, pride, fullness of bread, and abundance of idleness was in her and in her daughters, neither did she strengthen the hand of the poor and needy. And they were haughty, and committed abomination before Me, therefore I took them away as I saw good." Ezekiel 16:49*

Pride, prosperity and perversion were the trademarks of ancient Sodom and the other cities of the plain. God's wrathful judgment upon that whole society fell suddenly, and only a few who believed in the Lord escaped His sudden fury.

There is nothing sinful about having plenty of food to eat or even an abundance of pleasant things and leisure time. But, when pleasures and possessions become the full end of man, he becomes proud, greedy, and often very immoral. Perversion is only one step away from an immoral society. These were the downward steps that led to Sodom's destruction. This downward trend has gripped the land of the Stars and Stripes, and we are now plunging to the depths of filth and perversion. What a great tragedy for a people that once lived in the light of God's Word!

9.   FALLEN FOUNDATIONS

End-time Babylon will have lost her moral sense of direction – *"her foundations are fallen, her walls are thrown down . . ." (verse 15)*   When any nation begins to throw off restraint by outlawing the God of heaven and His laws, that nation faces unbelievable trials and just retribution.

This passage could also be referring to the destruction of the law of the land, our national Constitution. Today, through judicial tyranny, the "ultimate law of the land" as preserved in the U.S. Constitution is being nullified and trashed. If ever there was a need for a Constitutional Amendment, now is the time. No vote of the people should ever be overthrown by any branch of government. Truly, our national *"foundations are fallen!"*

People of faith should pray that the godly standards of the Bible will once again be welcome in our land.

10.   AGRICULTURAL GIANT

Babylon   will   be a great agricultural production center, but the day will come when the farmers will suddenly abandon their crops in the field and run in panic. *"Cut off the sower in Babylon, and him that handleth the sickle in the time of harvest; for fear of the oppressing sword they shall turn everyone to his own land." (verse 16)*

One day Jew and Gentile alike (as well as illegal immigrants who overflow the land) will flee from Babylon in sheer panic.   Even those living in rural areas, which are usually considered a refuge and place of safety, will someday run in terror. What a terrible picture of future mayhem.

11.   THE HAMMER OF THE EARTH

Babylon is referred to as *"the hammer of the whole earth." (Jeremiah 50:23)* End-time Babylon will be a nation that is a great manufacturing giant. Babylon will be a nation that works and gets things done. The hammer in this verse is not speaking of a destructive weapon but of a mighty hammer of production and tool of commerce and development.

America has been the hammer of development, not only in her own land, but around the world. Even nations that have declared war against the hammer of economic might have been rebuilt by their one-time enemy!

12.   STRIVING AGAINST THE LORD

Babylon will be characterized as a land that is *"striving against the LORD." (verse 24)* Liberal justices, legislators and educators have made every effort to expel God and His moral standards from our society. What a sad day it is when the silent majority is overwhelmed by outspoken, ungodly activists who want to outlaw God in every facet of public life.

13. STOREHOUSES

Jeremiah 50:26 refers to the many food *"storehouses"* of end-time Babylon. How many nations are there who have such an abundance of food kept in storehouses like America? Take a drive through the Midwest and count the grain elevators that are filled to overflowing with stored food reserves.

No other nation on earth has been so blessed that they can help feed the hungry, starving masses beyond their borders. When disaster strikes the world looks to America for a handout and we give it generously. We are, indeed, a land of countless "storehouses."

14. ARROGANT

Babylon will be a proud nation. National pride is one thing, but a haughty prideful spirit is hated by God. *" . . . she hath been proud against the LORD, against the Holy One of Israel." (verse 29)*

The people of end-time Babylon will exalt and deify man in the place of God. Humanism is now the accepted religion of the land. Our children are being taught to trust in themselves and the "system" because man thinks that he is able to determine his own destiny without the LORD.

15. MANY CITIES
Babylon will be a land of many *"cities" (verse 32)*. This verse all by itself should convince us that end-time Babylon is more than the forty-acre project of Saddam Hussein in rebuilding ancient Babylon!

An airplane flight at night across the land is all that it takes to remind us that America is truly a land of many cities. The lights of one city after another go on and on for hundreds of miles along both the eastern and western coasts. "Many cities" . . . truly an accurate description of our fast-growing nation.

16. A PEOPLE ON THE GO
Babylon will be a land with a fully developed transportation system and numerous roads. Verse 37 makes reference to their *"horses and chariots"* which is the term that an ancient prophet would use to describe modern vehicles of transportation.

17. MIXED MULTITUDE
Babylon will be made up of a mixed multitude. She will be the melting pot of the world. Verse 37 mentions the *"mixed people,"* and the word mixed is literally translated *"mongrel people"* or *"mixed race."* Millions of people from all over the world are flooding into the United States every year. It should be noted that the nations are not knocking down the doors trying to enter Iraq, the homeland of ancient Babylon. Obviously, the prophets were not speaking about old, historic Babylon, but about a young and vibrant melting pot of all nationalities.

18.   FEMINISM IN SOCIETY

"They shall become like women . . ." *(verse 37)* may be referring to the society becoming a feministic society. The feminists' agenda world-wide, but especially in the United States, is having a devastating impact upon the entire nation.

College campuses are beginning to complain about the decreasing number of male students. On many university campuses men are outnumbered by women nearly two to one. Little wonder! With the exorbitant cost of education, who wants to be continually lectured about the evils of manhood?

19.   TREASURES ROBBED

"A sword is upon her treasuries, and they shall be robbed." *Jeremiah 50:37*   Inflation continues to rob Americans of their wealth, to say nothing of the graduated income tax. We would recommend the book and tape *"The Creature of Jekyll Island"* by G. Edward Griffin as an excellent exposure of the Federal Reserve System which is not Federal any more than Federal Express is, but is a huge and powerful banking cartel of the largest banks in America and Europe. The central banking system that brought America the great depression continues to rob the land of its full economic wealth and potential.

Since our government abandoned the gold standard and opted for Federal Reserve Notes, Americans have been continually robbed of their treasures. It is interesting to note that President John F. Kennedy had just signed a presidential order reinstating the hard currency standard to back up the dollar when he was assassinated and Lyndon Johnson became president. Johnson's first act after being sworn in was to rescind the order before they even arrived back in Washington D.C. on the historic flight from Dallas. Silver reserves were then peddled to the Federal Reserve for five cents on the dollar.

20. DROUGHT

Verse 18 declares that *"a drought is upon her waters and they shall be dried up."* The effects of drought have been devastating to areas like Lake Powell, and even the Great Lakes. Babylon will not be free from the ravages of nature. We should be careful here to not interpret every dry spell as the direct fulfillment of Biblical prophecy. The point is, Babylon will experience natural disasters and droughts. This is surely not referring to a desert area like Iraq which experiences continual drought.

21. LAND OF INVENTIONS

Babylon shall be the land of many inventions -- . . . *it is the land of carved images, and they are mad over their idols."(verse 38)* Little needs to be added here about American ingenuity and creativity as we have led the world in inventions and technological development. In addition to being a land of idol worship, the people are obsessed with their possessions.

22. DAUGHTER OF BABYLON

The phrase *"daughter of Babylon"* is found in verse forty-two of this 50th chapter of Jeremiah. This obviously is referring to a younger descendant of Babylon and not to historic Babylon.

Jeremiah Chapter 51

23. GOLDEN CUP

Babylon is described as *"a golden cup in the LORD's hand." Jeremiah 51:7* This could be referring to the fact that God has richly blessed our land, and we in turn have been a blessing to others. No other nation has ever been so generous in feeding the poor, providing emergency relief and sending forth so many missionaries world-wide.

24. EVIL INFLUENCE

End-time Babylon is also accused of making the nations of the earth *"drunk." (Jeremiah 51:7)* The cultural and immoral impact of America upon the world is currently deplorable. America is leading the world in the production and printing of porn and filth. When you travel abroad you will be amazed at the impact of the filthy lyrics and the rancid "music" of MTV. I visited Russia several years ago and felt ashamed that the people were watching the worst of the entertainment industry that is produced in our land. While people from other countries enjoy our foul entertainment, their opinion of "Christian" America is that she is a land of moral pollution.

25. DWELLING UPON MANY WATERS

"Thou that dwellest upon many waters" (verse 13) probably refers to our many coastlands and ocean ports.

Our merchant marines fill the oceans as we import and export merchandise all over the world. The phrase could also refer to the political influence of America as we dispatch our countless ambassadors all over the globe.

It should be noted here that one of the greatest threats to our national security is the hundreds of thousands of metal shipping containers coming into our ports every year. The potential of terrorists shipping weapons of mass destruction right into the ports of our major cities is very real.

26.   A WEALTHY NATION

The phrase *"abundant in treasures" (Jeremiah 51:13)* is abundantly clear.   End-time Babylon will be wealthy beyond comprehension.   It is estimated that 7% of the world's population owns 50% of the world's wealth, and America has more than its share of millionaires. The LORD has blessed us abundantly for one reason – to spread the message of the Gospel to the entire world.

27.   INTELLECTUALLY STUPID

Verse 17 seems so ironic -- *"Every man is stupid by his knowledge."*   How can a person become stupid by knowledge? The fact is, *"the fear of the LORD is the beginning of wisdom."* Higher education without the knowledge of the LORD is vain and totally bankrupt.

The Bible declares that *"the fool hath said in his heart there is no God."* *(Psalm 14:1)* As a nation it seems that we have become a society of *"fools"* that cannot recognize that an intelligent design is the work of an "Intelligent Designer." The teaching of evolution as absolute fact and the denial of Biblical creation is undermining the entire educational system. There are social repercussions from removing God and His laws from society, and we are experiencing those social ills in today's world.

28. AGAINST ISRAEL

God refers to the *"evil that they have done in Zion."* *(Jeremiah 51:24)* On the surface, that couldn't possibly apply to the United States of America. After all, we have been one of Israel's most loyal friends. But, the fact is, in recent years our State Department has supported the Palestinians time after time as we have pressured the State of Israel to trade land for peace.

It would appear that every time we have sided against the people of Israel in giving up their God-given land for peace, some kind of natural disaster has occurred in our country. It may be more than mere coincidence that soon after we were involved with brokering the agreement to give the Gaza Strip to the Palestinians, we were faced with several severe hurricanes. God's promise to Abraham is still in effect – *"I will bless them that bless you and curse them that curse you."* *Genesis 12:3*

Who are we, or anyone for that matter, to give away the land that God claims as His own? Even Israel's leaders may have to learn that God's land is not theirs to barter away.

29.   PRAISE OF EARTH
Babylon is called *"the praise of the whole earth."* *(verse 41)* That was the testimony of the United Sates at one time. But this favorable view of the world toward America has become tarnished and drastically changed in recent years. No nation on earth has done so much for others and become so hated and despised. Much of the world's contempt may be of our own making, but some is completely unjustified as we are engaged in a life and death cultural war.

30.   IDOL WORSHIPPERS
God declared that He will *"punish Bel"* *(Jeremiah 51:44)* when He sends wrathful destruction upon Babylon. *"Bel"* refers to idolatry and Baal worship as we discussed in Chapter Two. As beautiful as the Washington Monument is, one wonders if it is an affront to the Lord by nature of what He knows it represents in the pagan world? Other evidences of the influence of idolatry are apparent throughout our society, especially in churches that have abandoned truth for idol-like symbols.

31. MOUNT UP TO HEAVEN

Jeremiah 51:53 is one of the most remarkable verses that describes end-time Babylon – *"Though Babylon should mount up to heaven . . ."* This verse could very well be referring to the remarkable ventures of the United States in space. America has led the way in the development of space travel and is the world's leader in modern technology and in the deployment of communication satellite systems. How incredible that we can take a trek into the wildest wilderness, check our location by G.P.S. and then use a cell phone to call home about it!

32. MILITARY STRENGTH

Jeremiah 51:53 continues -- *". . . and though she should fortify the height of her strength . . ."* This description may refer to the strength of our armed forces. It may also refer to the development of a space missile defense system. Whatever God means in this passage, we must not forget that He, and He alone, has been our strength and protector in the past. *". . . except the LORD keep the city, the watchman waketh but in vain . . ." Psalm 127:1b*

33. DRUNKEN LEADERSHIP

The next description is very sobering – *"And I will make drunk her princes, and her wise men, her captains, and her rulers, and her mighty men; and they shall sleep a perpetual sleep, and not wake, saith the King, whose Name is the LORD of Hosts." (verse 57)*

Alcoholism in the halls of congress is a national scandal. The drunkenness that prevails amongst many of our national leaders is alarming.

We learn from the Bible that *"perpetual sleep"* is another grave judgment that falls upon mankind when he forgets the God who created him. Man who boasts "I will not believe," soon "cannot believe."

> When people fail to give glory to the Creator, God gives them over to immorality. *(Romans 1:21-24)*

> When a nation fails to repent of immorality, God gives them over to perversion. *(Romans 1:26-27)*

> When a nation fails to repent of perversion, God gives them over to a reprobate mind. *(Romans 1:28)*

A *"reprobate mind"* is a mind that is incapable of making wise choices. It is a mind that is 180 degrees out of phase from the wisdom and counsel of God. The most insignificant decisions become continual blunders. This is the current spiritual condition of the United States.

Our public school system is an example of a nation incapable of making wise choices. Many young people graduating from high school cannot even read. Our answer to this problem is to invest more money and continue to convince youngsters there is no God and no right or wrong. We will have nothing to do with anything that remotely hints of the Judeo-Christian ethic and then wonder why we can't solve our social problems.

Isaiah chapter 13

The thirteenth chapter of Isaiah deals primarily with the final destruction of that great end-time land called "Babylon." We will deal with that in depth in another chapter. There are several phrases, however, which add to the clear descriptions of end-time Babylon.

34.   LAND OF INIQUITY

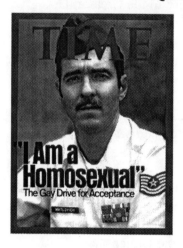

"I will punish the world for their iniquity." (verse 11) Babylon, along with many other nations, faces the judgment of God for its evil. We often think of Americans as the "good guys" . . . the nation that always wears a white hat.

There is no need to make an exhaustive list but, the sad fact is, evil prevails in the United States of America. The Mardi Gras is no Sunday School picnic, in case any of us have forgotten. That sensual celebration is considered the "heart and soul" of New Orleans. Should we then wonder why the city has been plagued with such horrendous problems?

The immorality and perversion that permeates our entertainment industry is a national disgrace. Our granting of special status, rights and privileges to sodomites is an affront to a holy God, and the slaughter of the innocent for the convenience of "don't wanna-be" mothers is a stench in the holy nostrils of the LORD Who is the LORD of Life. Then there is our preoccupation with magic and witchcraft which is frightening indeed. Need we go on?

35. NATIONAL ARROGANCE

The LORD declares – *"I will cause the arrogancy of the proud to cease, and will lay low the haughtiness of the terrible . . ." (verse11)* Nothing is more deplorable in the eyes of a holy and righteous God than pride and arrogance.

We have become a nation that has robbed God of the credit that is due Him because of all His blessings. The multitudes scoff at the importance of children praying and giving thanks to the God of Heaven. Ancient King Nebuchadnezzar once congratulated himself for the greatness of his kingdom and glory. You can read about his humbling experience of eating grass with the cattle of the field for seven years in *Daniel chapter 4.*

36. "GLORY OF KINGDOMS"

God refers to end-time Babylon as the *"glory of kingdoms."* What a wonderful title! There was a day when America stood for good and righteousness instead of perversion and wickedness. How tragic when "G" rated movies are shunned and destined to poor ratings before they even hit the movie theaters. Hollywood continues to create moral filth because that is what the public craves. If you want to determine the moral health of a nation, simply observe what entertains! What a tragedy that the *"glory of kingdoms"* will one day smolder in self-made destruction.

Isaiah Chapter 18

No actual reference to "Babylon" or the "daughter of Babylon" is made in Isaiah chapter 18. However, there are striking verbal descriptions that apparently apply to an end-time nation that sounds remarkably like America. These descriptions obviously apply to some great unnamed nation. You be the judge who the prophet was describing.

37.   SHADOWING WITH WINGS

"Woe to the land shadowing with wings." *(verse 1)* Is this a reference to the land whose national insignia is an eagle? It could be. But more likely it is referring to a land whose skies are filled with aircraft.

In the Hebrew language the word "shadowing" is actually translated "quivering," "rattling" or "vibrating." Speak to anyone who lives under the flight pattern of large commercial or military jets coming and going and ask them if their house ever vibrates or rattles. If their house doesn't rattle, their nerves probably do! No other nation on earth has the incredible amount of commercial air traffic as the United States.

I am an outdoorsman and I look forward to my annual hunting trek into the wilderness for a time of quiet and solitude. Any hunter can tell you that the peaceful silence of the Rocky Mountain back-country is broken by the sounds of jet aircraft. This is not a "once in a while" disturbance in the high country (or anywhere for that matter), but the noise of airplanes can be heard frequently throughout the day.

38. WEST OF JERUSALEM

Verse one of *Isaiah chapter 18* even pinpoints the location of the end-nation destined for judgment and destruction – *"beyond the rivers of Ethiopia . . . "*

God is describing a nation that is located to the west <u>beyond</u> Ethiopia. Ancient Babylon was east of Jerusalem, but this end-time nation is to the west, *"beyond the rivers of Ethiopia."* The Hebrew word "beyond" is better translated "over beyond." What a remarkable prophetic description of a nation beyond the seas!

39. MANY AMBASSADORS

"That sendeth ambassadors by the sea, even in vessels of bulrushes upon the waters . . ." *(verse 2)* Whoever this end-time nation is, it will be a nation that dispatches ambassadors and peacemakers all over the world. There should be little doubt which nation is the present world's "peacemaker." Somehow, it seems like we become embroiled in every conflict no matter where it occurs.

40. A SCATTERED NATION

"Go ye swift messengers to a nation <u>scattered</u> . . ." *(verse 2)* "Scattered" can be translated "planted and developed." This reference is to a country with great agricultural production, not to a country that is primarily a desert wasteland like so much of the Middle East and Iraq.

41. "DON'T TREAD ON ME!"

" . . . *to a people* <u>*terrible*</u> *from their beginning . . .*" *(verse 2)* In this passage, the ancient prophet was describing a people that are to be feared or respected. In the world's vernacular, the people of this end-time nation will be a people "not to mess around with!"

The military might and expertise of America has been displayed several times in Middle East conflicts. No nation on earth wants to go to battle against the well-trained and well-equipped American military forces. Nations that attacked our country during World War II will also attest to the fact that American forces are for real.

42. A NATION MEASURED OUT

" . . . *a nation* <u>*measured out*</u> *and trampled down . . .*" *(verse 2)* Measured out is thought by many to refer to a land that is plotted and mapped. The entire country is on detailed maps that show topographical elevations, private and public lands, buildings, governmental lands and easements, and the list goes on and on. Totally mapped . . . a good description of our land!

Dr. E.F. Webber commented on this in his book *"America in Prophecy"* –

"A nation meted out and trodden down." Or as it could be interpreted, "A land measured under foot." We learn from early history that at about the time Florida and Ohio were taken into the United States, a law was passed making it mandatory that all public land be surveyed by the North Star and divided into square mile sections, then subdivided into quarter sections, a half mile square, the size of a homestead. We were the first country ever to survey and divide the land according to the ranges with the North Star, and all our land from the western edge of Pennsylvania to the Pacific Ocean, and from Canada to Mexico, has been surveyed by lines of measurements, then staked out in quarter sections after this law of General Surveys had been passed. Now the prophet wrote about this twenty-seven hundred years ago, more than two thousand years before America was even discovered by Columbus. The prophet told about the fact that our land would be surveyed into sections whose lines point due north and south, east and west."

43.   A NATION TRAMPLED DOWN

"... *a nation measured out and* _trampled down_ ..." *(verse 2)* This undoubtedly refers to a land of many roads and highways. The interstate road system developed in the last 50 years began as a national defense network so that we could quickly and easily move troops to any spot in the nation, including Alaska. The first stretch of "National Defense Highway" was Interstate 70 in western Kansas and was named for then president Dwight Eisenhower. No other nation on earth has the roads and highways of our beloved land.

44. MANY RIVERS

"... *whose land the rivers have spoiled...*" *(verse 2)*
Some Bible scholars understand this to mean polluted rivers.
Others believe that this is referring to a land which has
become prosperous because of large rivers and the ability to
transport goods on the nation's waterways.

Actually, both definitions may apply because the rivers that
make America rich (such as the mighty Mississippi) are
polluted, in part, because of the commercial traffic of
countless barges and ships.

The mere existence of many rivers leads us to the
conclusion that the prophet was not referring to a vast desert
wasteland such as modern day Iraq, the land of ancient
Babylon. End-time Babylon will be a land characterized by
rivers filled with commercial traffic.

Isaiah Chapter 47

Isaiah chapter 47 is ripe with many descriptions of *"the
virgin daughter of Babylon."* The prophet begins the
chapter – *"Come down, and sit in the dust, O virgin
daughter of Babylon."*

There is little question as to whom this was directed – a
young end-time descendant of ancient Babylon.

45. A CALL FOR NATIONAL REPENTANCE

God calls out to the *"virgin daughter of Babylon."* *(verse 1)*
This is a call to repentance very similar to *Isaiah 1:18* –
"Come now, and let us reason together saith the LORD,

though your sins be as scarlet they shall be as white as snow; though they be red like crimson, they shall be as wool." The *"virgin daughter"* is probably an appeal to a nation that has experienced the Lord's protective care just as a father would protect and preserve the purity of his daughter. No one can doubt that the Lord Himself has protected and preserved our great land. The appeal to sit down in *"dust"* upon the *"ground"* is an obvious plea for national repentance.

46. INNOCENCE LOST

". . . thou shalt no more be called tender and delicate" *(verse1)* is an indictment against a nation who was once young and innocent and has now turned to sin and debauchery. Those of us who love our great land and know what it stood for in its inception are brokenhearted to see her abandon her godly foundation and roots.

47. NATIONAL EMBARRASSMENT

"Thy nakedness shall be uncovered, yea, thy shame shall be seen . . ." *(verse 3)* The purity of our land has been polluted by ungodly, dishonest and immoral leaders and representatives.

The Lord continues to allow all of our "dirty laundry" to be exposed to the world. A case in point was our recent president, Bill Clinton, and his sexual misconduct. The world jeers about the corruption of this so-called "Christian nation."

Recent scandals regarding our handling and holding of terrorists and prisoners of war are also big news to a world that loves to condemn the "ugly Americans." The tragedy is that these stories, whether true, false or exaggerated, come forth from the liberal American media with great glee and gloating.

48.   TARNISHED TESTIMONY

". . . for thou shalt no more be called the lady of kingdoms . . ." *(verse 5)* The testimony of moral integrity and purity will have become greatly blemished in end-time Babylon. America has become despised abroad, and often it is for good reason. Is that not a great tragedy?

Some have gone so far as to suggest that this reference to *"the lady of kingdoms"* could be speaking of our nation as depicted by our Statue of Liberty. Perhaps this is so, but I would personally hesitate to make this direct connection.

49.   SELF-CONFIDENT

"And thou hast said, <u>I shall be a lady forever</u>, so that thou didst not lay these things to thy heart, neither didst remember the latter end of it." (verse 7) End-time Babylon will be confident that her dress will never be wrinkled and that she cannot be brought down. As a nation, we are confident that we can handle anything that comes our way by pure determination and the American spirit. Such overconfidence is especially dangerous since our confidence

is no longer in the Lord Who has preserved and blessed us in the past.

50.   FUN CAPITAL OF THE WORLD

This description of end-time Babylon certainly fits the American life-style – *"thou are given to pleasures." (verse 8)*

No other nation on earth spends so much time, effort and money to be entertained. We are raising an entire generation of children who insist on the latest, most exciting and violent entertainment and video games. But, the fact is, their parents are no different. Fun and games reign!

Speaking of entertainment, restaurant chains have learned long ago that, if you want to sell burgers in America, you have to provide a fun atmosphere. That is not a criticism, just an observation of the way things are in the entertainment capital of the world.

51.   SAFE AND SECURE

"thou dwellest securely . . ." (verse 8) This Biblical phrase is without doubt referring to the security we enjoy within our country. We are blessed by having police and fire protection, to say nothing of well-trained and well-equipped

armed forces. Our public servants and military personnel are to be respected and thanked!

We have learned in recent years, however, that if the lights go out or if other disasters strike in our major cities, we need to find a place to hide. What a sad commentary that is of our land! Total anarchy, even in a country of well-established laws and enforcement, is only a step away.

52.   NO SORROW

" . . . *thou sayest in thine heart, I am, and none else beside me; I shall not sit as a widow, neither shall I know the loss of children." Isaiah 47:8*   Despite our losses in previous wars and even in the war against terrorism, we have never known the heartbreaking loss of an entire army fighting to defend our homeland.

President Bush reported to the nation on December 12, 2005, that we had lost over 2,000 of our brave soldiers in the fight against international terrorism and to liberate Iraq. At the same time, Iraq has experienced the loss of over 30,000 of their people in the war against tyranny and terrorism. We continue to lose our nation's finest young people, and each loss is a great tragedy, but we have not experienced again the huge heart-wrenching losses of World War II, nor have we experienced the horrors of an enemy invasion.

God pronounced judgment on Babylon in verses 9-11. Notice the reasons for coming judgment.

53.   BEWITCHED BY WITCHCRAFT

". . . *for the multitude of thy sorceries and for the great abundance of thine enchantments. . . " (verse 9)*

The Hebrew word for "sorceries" is literally "magic" or "witchcraft." Americans have become totally enamored with the likes of Harry Potter. The theme of witchcraft is also a major part of video games and children's cartoons which are capturing the minds and imaginations of an entire generation.

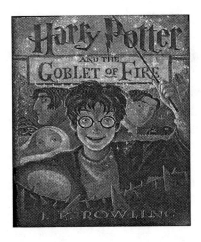

We have every reason to dread the future when we have abandoned spiritual values and embraced the occult. This is a very real problem on our school campuses where a growing number of students often dress in black and even wear black makeup as a symbol of their angry defiance and of the evil they openly embrace.

Infatuation with spiritual darkness and wickedness is justifiably, a great reason for alarm. Police officers will tell you that they are finding dead animals that have been mutilated and sacrificed in sadistic rituals. When this "game" matures, will children be at risk?

54. HIDDEN CRIME
"For thou hast trusted in thy wickedness; thou hast said, None seeth me." (verse 10) White collar crime is growing at an alarming rate. Computer and identity theft where would-be criminals think they can remain invisible is becoming more and more commonplace.

As I write I am listening to a television news report that sports fans seeking tickets to the Super Bowl are being stung on-line with pricy tickets that are bogus. The warning? Buy at your own risk! Why? Because crime is rampant. Our prisons are filled to overflowing. We have become a nation without a conscience.

27.   INTELLECTUALLY STUPID

This description is similar to #27 so the number is repeated. *"Thy wisdom and thy knowledge, it hath perverted thee; and thou hast said in thine heart, I am, and none else beside me." Isaiah 47:10*   Knowledge without acknowledgement of God is the goal of our public schools and universities. No wonder so many parents have opted for home-schooling.

Many parents are not aware until it is too late that their children have been negatively impacted by a humanistic worldview thrust upon them by liberal college professors. These teachers seem take special delight in shipwrecking the Biblical faith of their students.

55.   ATTACKED BY TERRORISM?

"Therefore shall evil come upon thee; thou shalt not know from where it riseth, and mischief shall fall upon thee; thou shalt not be able to put if off, desolation shall come upon thee suddenly, which thou shalt not know." (verse 11)

This passage could very well be a description of end-time terrorism. We now have numerous enemy terrorist cells living amongst us eagerly awaiting the opportunity to shed innocent blood and wreak havoc. When an attack comes, we will be confused as to who the real enemy is and where it came from.

This verse even declares *"thou shalt not be able to put it off, desolation shall come suddenly."* Terrorism thrives on the unsuspecting and ill-prepared. Our public leaders are even warning the public regarding future terrorists' attacks – "It is a matter of <u>when</u>, not if."

56.   TALK, TALK, TALK

"Thou are wearied in the multitude of thy counsels." (verse 13) End-time Babylon will apparently be the peacemaker of the world. Sometimes we all become weary of the unending rhetoric. Wherever or whatever the crisis, America is right in the middle of it. We have assumed the role of the "defenders of freedom," but sometimes it seems that America makes enemies by forcing ourselves into the center of every dispute.

57.   ASTROLOGY

"Let now the astrologers, the stargazers, the monthly prognosticators, stand up, and save thee from these things that shall come upon thee." (verse 13) It may surprise many people that our military leaders consulted mediums and astrological charts in selecting attack dates for many of the battles of World War II.

To this day, horoscope readings and mediums play a major role in what many Americans do and when they do it. In mockery, God challenges all these mediums to give direction for rescuing a nation now doomed to judgment.

58. ABANDONED BY HER FRIENDS
"Thus shall they be unto thee with whom thou has labored, even thy merchants, from thy youth; <u>they shall wander every one to his quarter</u>; none shall save thee." (verse 15)

This prophecy shall be more fully developed as we consider the destruction of Babylon in a later chapter. The prophets were simply   declaring that all of the merchants that bring goods to Babylon will abandon her when her day of calamity begins.

Revelation Chapter 18

Revelation chapter 18 in the last book of the Bible ties everything together. One of the primary messages of the prophecy relates to the horrible destruction of *"Babylon the great"* which takes place *"in one hour!"* The very mention of *"Babylon"* is proof positive that the prophetic words of the ancient prophets regarding Babylon are not yet all fulfilled.

59. LUXURIES AND ABUNDANCE
" . . . the <u>merchants of the earth are grown rich</u> through the abundance of her delicacies." (verse 3) Not only does this passage reinforce #58 above, that many foreign shippers and merchants will be trading with Babylon, this passage declares that they will *"become rich through the abundance of her delicacies."*   *"Delicacies"* is better translated "luxuries" in the Greek language. The merchants of the

earth will become wealthy because of the luxurious and consumptive life-style of the end-time Babylonians.

35. NATIONAL ARROGANCE
"How much she hath glorified herself, and lived luxuriously." *(verse 7)* This prophetic utterance again expresses the great spirit of pride and arrogance that will be a dark shadow over Babylon. She will boast of her great success and riches, not realizing that the God Who Provides is the One to whom all glory is due. He will not share His glory with anyone. Truly, pride cometh before a fall.

60. OVERCONFIDENT
Babylon will be at rest in overconfidence when her people declare – *"I sit a queen, and am no widow, and shall see no sorrow."* *(verse 7)* This self-confident spirit that "nothing bad can ever happen here" will be suddenly upended. "We can handle it" is the attitude of our entire nation, even as we careen down an immoral and reckless path that demands eventual judgment.

61. THE MONEY MAKERS
"And the kings of the earth who have committed fornication and lived luxuriously with her, shall bewail her and lament for her, when they shall see the smoke of her burning . . ." *(verse 9)* This divine utterance could be referring to the fact that America has made many nations and foreign leaders extremely wealthy.

Our State Department holds great sway over the nations through our gifts and financial assistance programs. Americans labor under an ever-increasing tax burden in order that our leaders can buy worldwide influence.

62.   THE GREAT CITY

" . . . *Babylon, that mighty city* . . . " *(verse10)* Just as London represents Britain, Paris represents France, and Moscow represents Russia, so the mere mention of a great city called "Babylon" will represent a huge and powerful end-time nation. If, in fact, Babylon does represent the United States of America, and no one can say absolutely dogmatically that it does, one wonders if that great city is New York . . . or Washington? Time will only tell which of the cities the prophet John had in mind.

One thing is for certain, when the fires of God's wrath and judgment fall upon end-time Babylon, many cities will be affected. *"I will kindle a fire in his cities, and it shall devour all round about him."* *Jeremiah 50:32*

63.   BROKEN-HEARTED SALESMEN

"And the merchants of the earth shall weep and mourn over her; for no man buyeth their merchandise any more . . . " *(verse 11)* What a reason to mourn – there is no one to buy their trinkets! This is another prophetic statement that the

merchants of the earth shall become rich through their business with end-time Babylon. It is common knowledge that if the consumption of America stopped, the economy of the entire world would suddenly collapse.

The point should be emphasized again – at the time of her destruction, end-time Babylon will be the greatest consumer of merchandise the world has ever seen.

64.   IMPORTS

Revelation 18:12-13 presents an extensive list of the *"merchandise"* consumed by Babylon. Examining that list of foreign-made products is quite revealing. It includes items that America now imports in great abundance such as gold, silver, precious stones, fine linen, ivory, precious woods, spices, perfumes, wines, and even <u>oil</u> and <u>iron</u>.

With all of the natural resources found in the United States, it is absolutely amazing that we import anything. But the price of labor has driven many American industries to either close or relocate their manufacturing shops to other countries, such as Mexico.

65.   IMPORTED IRON

Years ago, the United States was the steel producer of the world. Then steel companies like Bethlehem Steel in Pennsylvania and CFI in Colorado, and many others began to close.

Pictured above: A casting crew stands on the outside deck of Bethlehem Steel's last operating blast furnace on November 18, 1995, watching as the final batch of molten iron flows into a waiting submarine rail car. This cast ended iron-making in Bethlehem after more than 100 years at the plant which employed more than 30,000 men and women during World War II.

Now, after numerous other steel plants have closed, steel is one of our major imports from Japan. The Japanese are even huge importers of wood products as they buy raw materials from states like Alaska and turn it into profitable items like plywood. When my wife and I visited Alaska several years ago, I was amazed at the number of Japanese ships being loaded with wood chips which would be formed into plywood products and later resold in America.

66. OIL BY THE BILLIONS OF BARRELS

One of America's largest imports, of course, is oil. In the early months of 2006, America was importing over 14 million barrels of refined products and another 10 million barrels of crude oil each day.

Our dependence upon foreign imports in the area of energy may one day become the breaking point of the American economy, and even of our national defense.

67. CARS, CARS, CARS AND MORE CARS!

Of special interest is the end of *Revelation 18:13* where we read – " . . . *chariots, and slaves, and the souls of men.*"

God apparently showed the Apostle John the massive numbers of cars and vehicles that would one day choke the roads of Babylon. He called them "chariots" which was probably his only way of describing such strange vehicles.

Even more significant than the number of vehicles in "Babylon" is the fact that a huge number of these *"chariots"* would be manufactured and imported from other countries. The Apostle John prophesied that the merchants of the earth would grow wealthy from the vast number of products sold to "Babylon."

The automobile industry is a huge part of the American economy. But more and more cars on the roads are imports, and American auto workers face a very uncertain future.

The number of automobiles imported from Japan alone is absolutely staggering. This has taken a toll, of course, on the auto giants of America as more and more imports are being manufactured and imported into the U.S. Even American brand autos are being manufactured and assembled abroad. Jobs are being lost in states like Michigan and are being taken abroad and "south of the border."

68. SLAVERY

It is interesting that *Revelation chapter 18* also mentions *"slaves"* in this list of items bought and sold. One of the greatest blemishes to the testimony and reputation of our great land is the deplorable slave markets that once existed in America.

But this is also a present-day indictment upon Babylon for the purchasing and selling of human beings. Daniel Weiss from Focus on the Family wrote a commentary entitled "Porn Feeds Human Trafficking," published in the Denver Post, January 27, 2006 –

"Last week, President Bush signed the Trafficking Victims Protection Reauthorization Act of 2005, mandating the U.S. government and military expend greater efforts to combat the illegal practice of buying and selling human beings.

"As the president said at the bill-signing ceremony, 'Human trafficking is an offense against human dignity, a crime in which human beings, many of them teenagers and young children, are bought and sold and often sexually abused by violent criminals. Our nation is determined to fight and end this modern form of slavery.'

"The extent of the trade in human flesh is staggering. The U.S. Agency for International Development estimates that as many as 4 million people across the globe are bought and sold each year. Just within the United States, as many as 50,000 people are trapped in sexual slavery at any given time. This grim reality was again brought to light in a recent Toledo Blade series documenting how that city is a national trafficking hub for underage prostitution.

"The global tragedy hinges on the notion that human beings are commodities to be bought, sold, used and discarded. If the president is truly serious about ending the global sex trade, he would do well to start at home by cleaning up one of its primary drivers: the explosive growth of illegal hardcore pornography."

Weiss went on to add – *"Hardcore pornography, or material depicting actual sex acts, promotes the idea that human beings can be sexually used and abused without consequences. If we tolerate pornographic material that encourages people to indulge their darkest sexual fantasies, we cannot act surprised when millions do so in real life as well. In this regard, the United States is the world's worst violator."*

Weiss also reported that, according to the Adult Video News, 11,000 new pornographic films are released every year in the United States and web pornography has grown from 14 million Web pages in 1998 to over 260 million Web pages in 2003. The sale of innocent human beings continues in Babylon. What a national disgrace.

CONCLUSION
We have attempted to list all of the descriptions of end-time Babylon. Such a list is not all inclusive, but hopefully, the reader gets the point. According to the prophets, Babylon will be a great end-time nation that influences the whole world, and that nation is destined for destruction.

There is another source that should probably be added to the list. It is found along with the words of judgment coming upon Magog (Russia). I add the following to the list because I am convinced that the fire that falls upon Babylon will originate from the far north (more of that in chapter 4). The destruction of Babylon and Russia may be at the same time, which I personally believe will occur immediately after the "rapture," God's deliverance of born-again believers who trust in the Lord Jesus Christ as Savior and Lord. These horrendous events appear to occur just prior to, or at the beginning of, the seven years of Tribulation know as *"the time of Jacob's trouble"* in *Jeremiah 30:7.*

Ezekiel Chapter 39

"And I will send a fire on Magog, and among those who dwell securely in the coastlands; and they shall know that I am the LORD." Ezekiel 39:6

69.   MILITARY MIGHT
" . . . those who dwell securely . . ." End-time Babylon will be a mighty military power. To dwell securely means simply that the people have no fear of foreign invasion or distant armies. This description certainly fits the United States. No other nation on earth has such sophisticated

weaponry and a well-trained military.

70.   BEYOND THE SEA

" . . . *in the coastlands* . . ." This can be understood as "beyond the sea" or "farthest parts." The same Hebrew word is used in several interesting verses in conjunction with definitive locations - *Jeremiah 25:22 – " . . . the kings of the <u>coasts</u> which are <u>beyond the sea</u> . . ."*

> *Isaiah 41:5 – "The <u>coasts</u> saw it, and feared; the <u>ends of</u> <u>the earth</u> were afraid . . ."*

When destructive fires fall on Magog (Russia) they will apparently also descend upon the *"coastlands"* which are *"beyond the sea"* and at *"the ends of the earth."*

God does not provide such clear word pictures just to be ignored. There is a reason that He wants us to know that judgment will one day fall quickly. His purpose is not to cause terror, but to urge man to come into a proper relationship with Him through His Son, the Lord Jesus Christ. Do you know Him personally as Redeemer and Lord?

> *"But God showed His love toward us in that, while we were yet sinners, Christ died for us." Romans 5:8*

> *"For the wages of sin is death, but the gift of God is eternal life through Jesus Christ our Lord." Romans 6:23*

> *"For whosoever will call upon the Name of the Lord shall be saved." Romans 10:13*

BRIEF SUMMARY OVERVIEW

The Biblical Description of End-Time Babylon

The Bible describes a powerful end-time nation as *"Babylon"* and *"The Daughter of Babylon."* Babylon will be the youngest of great nations, born from a motherland, composed of a mixed multitude, a literal melting pot of all nationalities. Babylon is depicted as the most wealthy of nations, the world center of manufacturing, commerce, and agricultural production. Her location is to the west of Jerusalem, *"beyond the rivers of Ethiopia."* This end-time nation will also be the great consumer of the world's products with merchant ships filling her many harbors. The land will be fully developed and mapped with many cities. Air travel and military security are some of her greatest assets.

Babylon and her people, who once were recognized as the *"lady of kingdoms,"* will become preoccupied with pleasures, luxuries, and higher education. She will become arrogant in her attitude toward the Lord of heaven. She will give herself to drugs, occultic practices and great immorality. Perversion will become an accepted life-style. The sins of her national leaders will be exposed for all the world to see. The rumor of coming terrorism will cause multitudes to flee her cities and seek shelter in their own homelands. The once *"glory of kingdoms"* will come under the chastening hand of the Lord Who Himself made her great.

CHAPTER 4
HORDES FROM THE NORTH

President Roosevelt called it a "day of infamy." Every American young person and adult living on December 7, 1941, can recall exactly where they were and what they were doing when they first heard the shocking news – "Pearl Harbor Attacked!"

The Japanese raid on America's Pacific Fleet at anchor in Pearl Harbor came not only as a day of death and destruction, but it also came as a rude wakeup call to a peace-loving nation.

Before Pearl Harbor, Americans felt safe and untouchable, a long way from the war in Europe.

Not only was America taken by surprise on that fateful Sunday morning, but the nation woke up to the fact that she was far from ready to protect herself in a world of aggressive and dangerous enemies.

NEVER AGAIN!

America was suddenly thrust into World War II, and our national resolve became "never again." Never again would we be caught unawares! Never again would we be unprepared! Never again would an enemy inflict such devastation upon our peace-loving and unsuspecting people!

The sleeping American giant suddenly roused, and the nation prevailed.

TIME TO ARM

As a result of that fateful attack against our slumbering defenders, the post-war years of the 1950's and 60's brought about the greatest armament of any nation in history. The United States was serious about her resolve to prepare her military for any possible act of future aggression.

But America wasn't the only country arming itself. The Soviet Union was also building a huge military machine under the pretense of protecting itself from the aggressive dangers of the West.

Many of us remember the jitters of the "cold war" as many citizens took measures to protect themselves from they thought was an "unavoidable" war with the communists. I remember watching the husband of my third grade teacher build an underground concrete bunker in their backyard. They were getting ready for the ultimate "day of infamy." National defense and civil defense were absolute priorities in those days of cold war uncertainty. The world had entered the era where all-out warfare could reduce the entire planet to smoldering ashes in just a few moments' time. Such a nuclear nightmare is truly beyond comprehension.

During the next fifty years, leaders of the United Nations would make every effort to bring the world under the protective umbrella of the "New World Order" and a world-wide commitment to peace and disarmament.

PERESTROIKA

A day of relief, hope and victory flooded the free world with the dismantling of the Soviet Union and the onslaught of "perestroika." The evil empire of the Soviets had come to an end without firing a shot or launching a missile, and the world rejoiced.

Russia's newly adopted program of "openness" and the removal of the Berlin Wall gave the world additional hope that "peace and safety" were not only possible, but that they had finally arrived. Many of the world's leaders even boasted that we had entered the "Post-War Era."

Most Americans breathed a great sigh of relief that we were no longer living under the threat of annihilation and that the Russian war machine was being dismantled. Communism was finally dead, and the threat of nuclear holocaust was finally over. Or, so we were led to believe.

NOT ALL RUSSIANS AGREE

A former KGB policy planner by the name of Anatolly Golitsyn defected to the west in the late 1970's. In 1984 he published a book entitled *"New Lies for Old"* in which he claimed that the *"final, offensive phase"* of the Kremlin's plan to dominate the world would begin with the *"false liberation of Eastern Europe,"* the *"conversion of communism to democracy,"* and the *"demolition of the Berlin Wall."*

Every "change" we have witnessed in the former U.S.S.R., and even the "fall" of communism, was all part of a well-orchestrated master plan of deception as forewarned by Major Golitsyn six years before they began to occur. The purpose of this masterful deception, of course, would be to create an international atmosphere of peace and safety and to accelerate disarmament in the West.

TIME TO DISARM

Golitsyn's warnings fell on deaf ears, and as the United States boldly led the way into nuclear disarmament, Russia continued an incredible military build-up, and an even more incredible cover-up. According to Time Magazine, soon after the dismantling of the Berlin Wall, Russia increased its military spending to over 50% of its GNP. At the same time, America cut its military spending to 6%.

Before leaving office, President George H. Bush frantically made "deep concessions" in a last-minute effort to negotiate the START II disarmament treaty. American military bases all over the world were closed, and western missiles were dismantled even as the Russians accelerated their arms deployment.

As America became serious about disarmament, the Russians continued to launch many new nuclear powered submarines. These state of the art subs were produced in record numbers under the leadership of Russia's President Yeltsin. Each sub-marine was fully armed with dozens of nuclear warheads aimed at strategic military targets and population centers throughout the United States. Even now these undersea nuclear missile launchers are able to lurk off our shores with the ability to wreak havoc to our cities with little or no warning.

That's the reality of the "safer world" in which we live.

Russia's President Mikhail Gorbachev's earlier promise to convert weapons factories to manufacture peace-time products was nothing more than a hoax, but our media had convinced the American public that Russian intentions were truly honorable. Instead, Gorbachev increased the Russian military budget by a whopping 37%. Apparently this was the great contribution toward world peace that qualified Gorbachev to be awarded the 1990 Nobel Peace Prize.

Soon afterwards, the Kremlin also completed numerous deep underground civil defense structures around Moscow, each one of which is the size of the Pentagon. Meanwhile, the citizens of the United States continue to be exposed to an insane defense strategy known by the acronym "M.A.D." – "Mutual Assured Destruction." This simply means that we had agreed to abandon all civil defense plans and to scrap all anti-missile defense systems. Today Americans are still exposed to the threat of nuclear extinction because what few anti-missile systems we once had were scrapped and dismantled at the insistence of our liberal politicians.

Ask any person on the street where they would go in the event of a nuclear attack, and they wouldn't have a clue. The fact is, there are no civil defense sites posted or available.

As the new millennium dawned, the frantic efforts to deploy a STAR WARS missile defense system were plagued with failures, budget woes and setbacks, leaving the American public at incredible risk. As we have submitted to the conditions of disarmament treaties, the Russians have installed elaborate missile protection systems around their major cities.

These problems persisted up to the current time as reported by the United Press on January 19, 2006:

> Fort Greely, Alaska - "Behind the heavy barbed wire at this snowy range are silos containing eight interceptors designed to shoot down incoming enemy missiles. There were supposed to be sixteen in place by now. But after an embarrassing series of test failures in the ambitious, expensive and highly criticized program to build a national missile-defense shield, the U.S. military is slowing the deployment of interceptors while it

conducts more testing. The government has spent about $100 billion on missile defense since 1983, including $7.8 billion authorized for the current fiscal year.

"Interceptors, however, have failed five times in 11 tests, even though some critics of the program say the tests have been practically rigged to succeed."

Years ago, General Sir Walter Walker, former NATO Commander-in-Chief, issued his concern about the demise of NATO, the disarmament of the West and the Russian build-up:

"I consider it my duty, as a former NATO Commander-in Chief, to tell you of the extremely dangerous threats that lie ahead. It is because I know for certain that we are now in a period of the greatest <u>strategic deception, perhaps in all history</u>, that I feel I should not allow this occasion to pass without warning you of the future that lies ahead in the next decade."

General Walker saw the Russian Bear preparing for war. His warning continued:

"Despite the collapse of the Soviet economy, the Kremlin, under pressure from the military, is actually increasing the military budget by $42 billion to more than $160 billion. In contrast, only $7.5 billion is being earmarked for education, and a mere $4.5 billion for health . . . the Soviet Union is NOT on the verge of collapse. Western defense, on the other hand, is."

The Russians are excellent and patient chess players and masters of deceit. What's worse, our leaders have applauded every lie that has come out of the Kremlin. But, as they talked peace, the Russians continued to prepare for war.

20th CENTURY TROJAN HORSE

The fact is, the West has been lulled to sleep by the most brilliant scheme of deception the world has witnessed since the Trojan Horse. The giant Bear of the north may appear to be taking a peaceful nap, but the purpose of Russian hardliners continues to be world domination. The present generation of Americans has long forgotten the nauseating statement of Nikita Khrushchev:

"I dream of the hour when the last Congressman is strangled to death on the guts of the last preacher – and since Christians seem to love to sing about the blood, why not give them a little of it? Slit the throats of their children and drag them over the mourner's bench and the pulpit, and allow them to drown in their own blood; and then see whether they enjoy singing these hymns."

This gruff rhetoric of the 1960's has given way to a much more appealing, smiling and conciliatory leadership in Russia. For the past fifteen years they have opened their doors to a guarded form of free trade and have even taken on the guise of democracy. But the fact remains, the basic leadership of the nation has not changed, nor has their stated purpose for a global empire. The significant fact is that the sophisticated Russian missile and nuclear weapon systems have never been downsized or dismantled.

Meanwhile, the West has fully bought into the peace-loving propaganda of the Kremlin. Almost without exception, the people I talk to believe the threat of nuclear warfare has been all but removed. These are days of "peace and safety" in the opinion of most Americans. They sincerely believe that the threat of a full-scale nuclear exchange has been eliminated through the political process.

Perhaps the most distressing part of this plot of Russian "disinformation" and deception is that KGB lies are being successfully pedaled to our gullible public by our own media. The liberal American news makers seem to be major partners in a massive campaign to escalate our own disarmament despite unbelievable risks.

ULTIMATE VOICE OF AUTHORITY
The observations and warnings of military leaders and men in the know seem to be falling on deaf ears throughout the free world.

But there is ONE VOICE that speaks with absolute authority regarding the future events of planet earth, and we would be wise to listen before it is irreversibly too late.

That voice is none other than the voice of God as He speaks through His Word, the Bible.

In previous chapters, we have attempted to show that the Scriptures are filled with words of prophetic significance and warnings for the days in which we live. God, through His spokesmen, the prophets, has made every effort to publish His warnings for the end-time nation referred to as the *"daughter of Babylon."* This youngest, most wealthy and powerful nation on earth will be destroyed in just one hour, and the consuming fires will descend from the far north.

It is not mere speculation that the enemy to the north is a huge and powerful multi-national force led by *"Magog,"* which is recognized by most Bible scholars to be Russia.

PEARL HARBOR II

Despite America's resolve to never again be taken by surprise, the horrific events of 9/11 proved that no nation is safe by mere military might, intelligence networks or vigilance.

The blatant calls for the destruction of Israel and America by militant Islamic heads of state, religious leaders and terrorists is chilling indeed. Add to that the availability of portable weapons of mass destruction, and you have the perfect formula for unprecedented days of peril. When these weapons fall into the hands of hateful extremists and mad men, they will eventually make their way to our cities, and the world will never be the same.

In *Ezekiel chapter 38*, the prophet described the huge military might of Russia and her end-time allies which will consist of many Islamic nations. We believe this to be a present-day coalition of nations who have one common goal, the elimination of the State of Israel and the United States.

The prophets were very specific in declaring there was coming an attack from the north against the end-time *"daughter of Babylon"* –

> *"For, lo, I will raise and cause to come up against Babylon, <u>an assembly of great nations from the north country</u>, and they shall set themselves in array against her; from there she shall be taken; <u>their arrows shall be as of a mighty expert man; none shall return in vain.</u>"* *Jeremiah 50:9*

Jeremiah's declaration that the *"daughter of Babylon"* will be attacked from the north causes us to turn our attention to the prophecies that were written against that northern kingdom called *" the land of Magog."*

HERE COMES RUSSIA

Ezekiel chapters 38 and 39 are filled with details regarding the northern confederacy that will invade the Middle East (Israel) and be destroyed by divine judgment.

Just as the LORD had declared that He would bring destruction upon the *"daughter of Babylon,"* so He utters the same curse upon the northern enemy of His people Israel – *"Son of man, set thy face against Gog, of the land of*

Magog . . . . and say, Thus saith the Lord GOD; Behold, I am against thee, O Gog." Ezekiel 38:3

Later in this prophetic chapter of future wrath, God states His great displeasure with *Gog* when they lead a huge invasion against God's land, the land of Israel –

> *"And it shall come to pass at the same time when Gog shall come against the land of Israel, saith the Lord God, that <u>my fury shall come up in my face</u> . . . surely <u>in that day will there be a great shaking in the land of Israel</u>, So that the fish of the sea, and the fowls of the heavens, and the beasts of the field, and all creeping things that creep upon the earth, and the men that are upon the face of the earth, shall shake at my presence, and the mountains shall be thrown down, and the steep places shall fall, and every wall shall fall to the ground. And I <u>will call for a sword against him throughout all my mountains, saith the Lord God; every man's sword shall be against his brother</u>." Ezekiel 38:18-21*

It would appear that this portion of the prophecy is specifically directed against the invading armies from the north. When they enter "God's land," judgment will fall. I believe this will be a supernatural intervention wherein God will bring about great confusion amongst the invaders, and they will turn upon one another just as they did in the days of ancient Judah when God caused a huge army to utterly fall by the infliction of their own swords *(2 Chronicles chapter 20.)* That ancient battle was fought by the LORD of Hosts, the King and LORD of the people of Judah. It took King Jehoshaphat and his army three days to collect the spoils from the dead bodies. The people knew that this was a battle won by the LORD, because the fight was over before one of God's people could even draw his sword.

DEFEAT OF THE RUSSIAN ARMY

The Lord will once again intervene directly into the affairs of His covenant people, and the battle against the invading army from the north may be a repeat of previous victories of the LORD against the enemies of Israel.

Two interesting points should be made here:

> 1. The bodies of the invaders will be buried in the mountains <u>east</u> of the Dead Sea. These mountains are in the present-day country of Jordan – *"And it shall come to pass in that day, that I will give unto Gog a place there of graves in Israel, the valley of the travelers <u>on the east of the sea</u>; and it shall stop the noses of the travelers, and there shall they bury Gog and all his multitudes; and they shall call it the Valley of Hamon-gog." Ezekiel 39:11*

> Let us not forget that God has claimed all of the land from the River Egypt (Nile) to the River Euphrates which flows through the center of present day Iraq. The actual battle and destruction of Gog's invading army will apparently take place east of present day borders of Israel.

> 2. God will only destroy 83% of the invading army – *"And I will turn thee back, and leave but the sixth part of thee, and will cause thee to come up from the north*

*parts, and will bring thee upon the mountains of Israel."
Ezekiel 39:2*

This overwhelming, but partial victory, may give opportunity for the coming world dictator, known as anti-Christ, to become involved, win an easy victory over the remaining survivors from Gog's northern army and thereby win the confidence of the Jews who expect to recognize their Messiah when he saves them from the northern invasion. The deceiver will declare himself to be their long-awaited Messiah, and after three and one half years he will turn on them, desecrate their Temple in Jerusalem and demand their worship.

RUSSIA'S SMOLDERING HOMELAND

In addition to the decisive victory over the invading forces in the land of Israel, God is going to call for the destruction of Russia's homeland as we read in *Ezekiel 39:3 and 6 – "And I will smite thy bow out of thy left hand, and will cause thine arrows to fall out of thy right hand . . . And I will send a fire on Magog, and among those who dwell securely in the coastlands."*

God will personally intervene against the army of Gog, and they will fall upon the mountains of Israel. At the same time, the Russian homeland will also be destroyed as God calls for fire against them. This just judgment against the land of Russia could very well be the retaliatory response of another nation that becomes embroiled in the catastrophic melee. In all probability, the *"daughter of Babylon"* will be able to send a fiery response during the time of her own destruction. Notice that *"I will smite thy bow out of thy left hand, and will cause thine arrows to fall out of thy right hand . . ." (verse 3)* The Russian homeland and the bases for her remaining weapons will apparently feel the retaliation of nuclear weapons. That's the theory behind M.A.D. (Mutual Assured Destruction). The aggressor may ultimately "win" the war but will pay a horrific price.

Regardless of the possible scenario, we do know that end-time Babylon will be attacked from the north and be totally annihilated. Possibly during the same conflict the Russian homeland will suffer great destruction, and the Russian forces invading the land of Israel will be humbled.

There is something else very interesting to note in all of this -- during this massive battle there will be a *"shaking in the land of Israel, so that the fish of the sea, and the fowls of the heavens, and the beasts of the field, and all creeping things that creep upon the earth, and all the men that are upon the face of the earth, shall shake at my presence . . ."* *Ezekiel 38:20* This will be no small military action limited to a tiny area like Israel. This conflict will be international in scope, and even the *"fish of the sea"* will suffer the consequences in what apparently will be an all-out nuclear warfare.

When the Lord specifically mentions *"a shaking in the land of Israel,"* one would speculate that this shaking could be describing weapons of mass destruction being detonated somewhere east of present-day Israel but still within the boundaries of what He calls "His land." This *"shaking"* could include the final melting down of Saddam Hussein's rebuilding effort of the ancient city of Babylon.

One would wonder why this day of calamity will also involve the *"fish of the sea."* Is it possible that at the same time God is delivering a death blow to the invading Russian hordes, that there is another even larger battle taking place that would include nuclear explosions at sea?

We do know that nuclear weapons would be employed against enemy submarines in an all-out thermonuclear exchange. Time will tell how this passage will be literally fulfilled. It is always easier to observe the exact meaning of prophetic utterances after they have been fulfilled.

We cannot help but ask, "Just who will comprise this massive invading army that comes against the land of Israel?"

ISLAMIC JIHAD

When *"Gog of the land of Magog"* invades the land of Israel, he will have amassed a huge confederacy of nations intent on annihilating Israel once and for all. In today's world, if Russia decided it was time to launch a full-scale attack against Israel, she would have plenty of Moslem volunteers who would be overjoyed to take part in destroying their mortal enemy.

The nations in league with the king of the north are listed in *Ezekiel 38:4-6* – *"And I will turn thee back, and put hooks into thy jaws, and I will bring thee forth, and all thine army ... Persia, Cush,*

and Put with them; all of them with shield and helmet; Gomer, and all its hordes; the house of Togarmah of the north quarters, and all its hordes; and many peoples with thee."

An author and student of the prophetic scripture, Mark Hitchcock, spent considerable time and effort in researching the names and identities of the nations that invade Israel with Russia. In his book, *"After The Empire,"* he summarized his findings:

"Three of the invaders of Ezekiel 38 and 39 have now been identified: the former southern Soviet republics, the former Russian republic and Turkey. The former southern Soviet republics and Turkey have almost everything in common – language, religion, political ties, economic compatibility, and, of course, a common Moslem hatred of Israel. It's not too difficult to imagine these two getting together in the near future to invade Israel." (Chapter 4, pages 50-51)

We may be surprised that Turkey is listed as one of the nations in league with "Magog," or Russia. Modern-day Turkey seems to have strong ties to the West, but those ties are purely economic. Even during the second conflict with Iraq, the Turks prohibited the United States from having air bases in their land. Their allegiance to the Moslem world cannot be underestimated.

In addition to Turkey and the five former Soviet republics of Kazakhstan, Uzebekistan, Kirghizian, Tajikistan, and Turkmenistan (all Islamic republics), Hitchcock researched these additional Moslem nations that will be partners with

Russia in the invasion of Israel:

> "Persia" is modern-day Iran.

> "Cush" is modern-day Sudan, south of Egypt and under the control of militant Islam.

> "Put" is modern-day Libya who has already illustrated its hatred for the West and Israel in particular.

The Prophet Ezekiel apparently did not list all the nations that will be involved in this action against Israel since we read in *Ezekiel 38:6, 9 and 15* – " . . . *many peoples with you.*" One of the nations Ezekiel does not list is *"the king of the south,"* referring to Egypt, but Egypt is listed as one of the participants in this great invasion by the Prophet Daniel in *Daniel 11:40-43.*

One nation in particular deserves a special comment, and that nation is Iran. Iran has been identified as ancient "Persia." A majority of the extremist militant warfare being waged by the Muslim world is coming right out of Iran. Iran is financing Hamas in their effort to destroy Israel. Also, Iran is very involved in much of the suicide bombing that is taking place in Iraq. Iran has been personally behind many of the attacks that have been waged against American forces such as the destruction of the Marines' barracks in Beirut, Lebanon, in 1983, when 241 American service men were killed.

Near the end of the Iran-Iraq war, Ayatollah Khomeini was able to send hundreds of thousands of young men against the well-armed forces of Saddam Hussein. Many of these young men were armed only with knives and copies of the Koran. Multiplied thousands were killed as wave after wave of these suicide attackers faced the machine guns of the Iraqi army. But they caused such panic amongst the Iraqi invaders that the battle was won by Iran and Saddam's forces retreated.

This same type of frenzied militiamen may one day mount a similar attack against the people of Israel when the multitude of Islam join forces with Russia and attempt to drive the Jews into the Mediterranean Sea.

THE SPARK THAT IGNITES THE HOLY WAR
It is obvious that a gigantic horde of Islamic warriors will one day become embroiled in their hatred against Israel. Hatred for the people of Israel has burned in the hearts of Muslims for many hundreds of years. But something will incite them to quit fighting amongst themselves, unite and join forces with the Russian army to march into the Holy Land.

We need to consider these questions:

> **What is the spark that will agitate the Muslim world so much that their Islamic armies will unite and join Russia in invading Israel?**
>
> **Is there any way to determine when such a day of infamy will begin?**

It is possible that the people of Israel will one day soon locate the Ark of the Covenant which was placed into hiding before the destruction of Jerusalem by Nebuchadnezzar in 586 B.C.

There are already ultra-orthodox Jews ready to break ground for their new Temple, and the finding of the ancient instruments of the Temple would add fuel to their zealous desire to re-establish ancient Temple sacrifices.

Such findings could fuel an all-out Holy War from the Muslim world, especially if something happened to the Dome of the Rock which stands on the site of Solomon's Temple. These events could quickly lead to the invasion from the north as envisioned by Jeremiah.

CHAPTER 5
THE BLASTING CAP OF
WORLD WAR III

HOOKS IN THE JAWS

When Jeremiah the prophet declared that God would *"put hooks into thy jaws" (Jeremiah 38:4)*, it would appear that the invasion of Israel will become so tempting that the massive armies from the far north simply cannot resist. These irresistible "hooks" could possibly be an economic prize so great to *"Gog of the land of Magog"* that he is compelled to take the ultimate risk despite the objections of other nations.

The Prophet Ezekiel tells us exactly why Russia would send her forces into the land that God calls His own –

> *"And thou shalt say, I will go up to the land of unwalled villages; I will go to those who are at rest, who dwell safely, all of them dwelling without walls, and having neither bars, nor gates, <u>to take a spoil</u>, and to take a prey; to turn thine hand upon the desolate places that are now inhabited, and upon the people that are gathered out of the nations, who have gotten cattle and goods, who dwell in the midst of the land. Sheba and Dedan, and the merchants of Tarshish, with all its young lions, shall say unto thee, <u>Art thou come to take a spoil?</u> Hast thou gathered thy company to take a prey, <u>to carry away silver and gold, to take away cattle and goods, to take a great spoil?</u>" Ezekiel 38:11-13*

STARK CONTRAST

If you ever have the opportunity to travel to Israel and other countries in the Middle East, you will be amazed at the incredible difference between Israel and all her neighbors. The contrast is striking! In the Jewish areas of Israel, the well-kept appearance of houses and neighborhoods, the condition of roads and the overall upkeep of the entire community, all speak of a modern country where the people are taking great pride in their nation. Across the border from Israel in any direction is dirt and disarray. I am not trying to be unkind, but the contrast is truly remarkable. To illustrate this, visit the city of Eilat, Israel, and then cross the border into Amman, Jordan, or take a day trip into Egypt. The same contrast can even be seen right within the city limits of Jerusalem.

The greatest prize, of course, for a massive invasion is more than beautifully developed communities and well-maintained infrastructure. The real prize may even be more than the wealth of the Dead Sea, and more than the combined wealth and assets of all the Israelis. The real prize for *"Gog of the land of Magog"* is probably the incredible wealth of the entire Persian Gulf and the warm sea ports that accompany it. Remember, this massive area with its wealth and oil reserves, is all part of the land promised to Abraham – *"In the same day the LORD made a covenant with Abram, saying, Unto thy seed have I given this land, from the river of Egypt unto the great river, the river Euphrates." Genesis 15:18*

Whatever the *"great spoil"* is, Russia will be part of a huge military force that will invade and overflow the ancient lands of Israel. Russia has always been a great opportunist.

In history they have often created a crisis to which they respond for the purpose of strategic gain. It is possible that their obsession with world control will one day cause them to invade *"God's land."*

But why would the Islamic nations join in such a reckless venture? They already control the vast oil reserves of the Persian Gulf.

BLASTING CAP OF THE MIDDLE EAST

The Middle East is a dangerous powder keg that could erupt into a scene of terrible bloodshed and death at any time. Without doubt, Israel is the blasting cap that could cause that powder keg to blow at a moments' notice!

It is obvious from the Scriptures that hordes of Islamic warriors will one day become so embroiled in their hatred toward Israel that they will attempt to penetrate her borders.

What could cause such hatred to come to a boiling point?

THE SPARK THAT IGNITES THE POWDER KEG OF ISLAMIC HATRED

There may be several situations that could cause the Islamic world to forget their differences and become organized in their attempt to exterminate the State of Israel:

1.   AN ISARELI MILITARY ATTACK

In January, 2006, the Iranian government announced their intentions to enrich nuclear materials for the "peaceful" purpose of generating electricity. The project is a joint-effort between Iran and Russia. Russia has already installed the necessary equipment at the Natanz nuclear complex in Iran, and they have many of their own technicians there to oversee the work.

**Extremist Iranian President,
Mahmoud Ahmadinejad**

The recent Iranian announcement of their nuclear intentions and their refusal to comply with international on-site nuclear inspectors has brought many protests and much concern from nations in the west. Iranian President, Mahmoud Ahmadinejad, has declared his open hatred for and desire to see Israel eliminated from the world.

Israel, of course, cannot allow such a fanatical and rogue state to gain nuclear weapons as their entire country would be at immediate risk of annihilation. If no other country intervenes, Israel may have no recourse but to use military force in destroying the nuclear capabilities of Iran or any other terrorist nation. This act of self-defense could obviously be a trigger that could ignite a greater conflict with the Muslim world. According to the prophetic scriptures, Russia will be involved.

But there are other factors that could bring the Islamic world together in a determined move to destroy their Israeli enemies.

2.   EFFORT TO BUILD THE "THIRD TEMPLE"
There is a growing movement in Israel to rebuild the Temple and to re-establish the ancient temple sacrifices. Preparations are even now underway by the Temple Mount Faithful in the training of priests and the breeding of sacrificial animals, namely the red heifer.

The mere idea of rebuilding the Jewish Temple is not well received by Moslems anywhere in the world. The events that surrounded the Palestinian riot at the Temple Mount several years ago is an example of the explosive nature of any attempt to build a Third Temple in Jerusalem. Many of the facts related to the Temple Mount Riot are not known by most of the public. World Daily News reported the following on August 1, 2001 –

"A group of religious Jews attempt to place a cornerstone for a Third Temple on Temple Mount. Every year, Gershon Salomon applies for the necessary permits from the Israeli government. Every year, his group is refused permission. Salomon's group, known as the Temple Mount Faithful, carries the four-ton cornerstone as close as they are allowed to go. And each year, huge rocks and chunks of concrete rain down on the worshippers at the Western Wall from 70 feet above."

In addition to the desire of the Temple Mount Faithful to build another Temple, there is another situation that could bring the whole issue to an explosive head. It is possible that the Ark of the Covenant will be located and will be unearthed in the future.

3. LOCATION OF THE ARK OF THE COVENANT

The locating of the ancient Ark of the Covenant would greatly accelerate the interest of Jewish people from all over the world in rebuilding their Temple.

It is common knowledge that the original Ark of the Covenant was removed from Solomon's Temple sometime before 586 B.C. when the Temple and the city of Jerusalem were destroyed by the Babylonian armies of King Nebuchadnezzar.

Just where was the sacred Temple furniture hidden in the days before the fall of Jerusalem? This is a question that has caused many modern-day adventurers to go on extensive "treasure hunts."

The locating of the ark has even been the topic of the Hollywood film industry with the production of "Raiders of the Lost Ark," speaking of which, we can be reasonably confident that the Ark of the Covenant is NOT in the National Archives of the United States!

Some claim that the ark was safely taken out of the country long before Nebuchadnezzar attacked the city of Jerusalem and that it now resides in a church somewhere in Ethiopia. Others believe that an ark in Ethiopia is but a copy of the original. Still others claim that the ark is still hidden in tunnels deep below the original Temple, on or near Mount Moriah in Jerusalem.

Ron Wyatt, a famed archeological explorer, became involved in trying to solve the mystery of the lost Ark of the Covenant. His claims are especially interesting so we will give a little background of this man and how he apparently won the respect of Jewish authorities interested in ancient antiquities in and around the city of Jerusalem.

INTERESTING ARCHEOLOGICAL DISCOVERIES
Wyatt is credited with numerous significant discoveries including the possible locating of Noah's Ark near the slopes of Mt. Ararat in Turkey. After an article printed in Life Magazine in 1960 showing strange satellite pictures of a boat-shaped object, Wyatt made the first of many trips to the area and conducted many scientific studies.

Boat-shaped object near Mt. Ararat in Turkey

There are many critics of Wyatt's research and discoveries in Turkey, but it seems significant that archeologists in Turkey have done research on their own and, as a result of their findings, the Turkish government has opened a Visitors Center at the site. The area has been dedicated as "Noah's Ark National Park" and designated a National Treasure.

I felt that the claims of Wyatt deserved more investigation so I traveled south of Nashville to Cornersville, Tennessee, in February 2006 to meet Wyatt's widow, Mary Nell Wyatt-Lee. I was invited to visit the home of Mary Nell and her new husband, and they treated me with great kindness.

I was surprised when she revealed that I was one of the few Christian men who had bothered to come to see the evidence for themselves and to ask questions. She was dismayed that none of her husband's critics had ever bothered to come and probe into the truthfulness or accuracy of his research.

I was also quite surprised that they showed me two of the artifacts taken from the probable Ark site. The first was a heavy piece of fossilized wood that revealed three layers of timber laminated together into a single beam. It was probably a broken piece of decking or possibly a small structural beam.

The remarkable thing is that the specimen was found by ground radar on the very day that Turkish dignitaries had assembled to officially dedicate the site, June 20, 1987. Wyatt had been restricted from digging at the site. However, Turkish Governor Ekinci was so intrigued at the data revealed by a demonstration of the ground radar unit, that he ordered his men to dig up the piece of fossilized wood which proved to be a tremendous find. Whatever the specimen is, it was obviously man-made.

Mary Nell Wyatt-Lee and the author holding the broken laminated wood beam found at the probable Noah's Ark site in Turkey.

The huge boat-like object in Turkey reveals an overall length of 515 feet, or exactly 300 Royal Egyptian Cubits, which would have been the measurement used by Moses, the writer of the Book of Genesis. Surely that is more than a coincidence!

I was also shown another interesting artifact which appeared to be a metal rivet and plate. This should not surprise us in that *Genesis 4:22* declares that men were *"craftsmen in bronze and iron"* long before the flood in Noah's day.

Whatever the object was, it was obviously a man-made artifact.

The book, *"The Boat-Shaped Object on Doomsday Mountain,"* written by Wyatt's widow, Mary Nell Wyatt-Lee, is an excellent resource that answers many questions and removes all doubts in my mind regarding the authenticity of the Ark. It is available from Wyatt Archeological Research at 2502 Lynnville Highway, Cornersville, TN, 37047.

Ron Wyatt is also credited with locating the Red Sea crossing site at Neweiba Beach which is approximately 40 miles south of Eilat, Israel. Evidence of this remarkable Find is detailed in the fascinating book, *"The Exodus Case,"* by Dr. Lennart Moller.

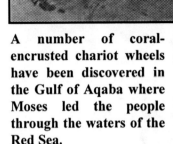

A number of coral-encrusted chariot wheels have been discovered in the Gulf of Aqaba where Moses led the people through the waters of the Red Sea.

Soon after finding evidence of undersea chariot parts off the shores of Neweiba Beach, Egypt, Wyatt entered Saudi Arabia and located what appears to be the real Mount Sinai.

The Split Rock at Horeb (left) where water gushed forth for the thirsty Hebrew people in the desert.

Remnants of the twelve columns erected by Moses at Mt. Sinai (right). Pictures courtesy of Wyatt Archeological Research.

In harmony with *Galatians 4:25,* Mt. Sinai is located in the ancient land of Midian which is modern day Saudi Arabia.

Egyptian *petroglyphs* of bulls located at what appears to be the Golden Calf Altar at Mt. Sinai in Saudi Arabia.

Wyatt also documented the "five cities of the plain" destroyed in the days of Lot. Up until his investigation most other researchers assumed the cities were under the Dead Sea. The fact is, they are in plain sight, and the best preserved ruins are thought to be the ancient city of Gomorrah which is located right at the foot of Masada. You can visit the site and find the sulfur pellets in many locations just as Wyatt claimed.

One can't help but wonder why one man would be instrumental in finding so many archeological sites that are of such great Biblical significance. Without a doubt, the Lord had a purpose in allowing him to make so many of these discoveries.

CREDIBILITY FOR A GREATER FIND?

Perhaps God Himself was giving Wyatt the credibility he would need to work under the watchful eye of the Department of Antiquities and governing officials in the State of Israel. Was there an even more significant "find" yet to be revealed?

Before his death in 1999, Wyatt worked for over ten years in an area outside the city walls known as the Calvary Escarpment. The site is located near the Damascus Gate and just north

Golgotha, the place of the skull.

of the walls of Jerusalem. His excavations took place within several hundred feet of the Garden Tomb where we believe Jesus Christ was buried for three days before He was resurrected.

During Wyatt's expedition at the Garden Tomb, he also discovered an iron rod that had been apparently drilled into the face of the tomb by Roman soldiers to seal the burial place of Christ. They had been instructed by Pontius Pilate

— "Ye have a watch; go your way, make it (the tomb) *as sure as ye can. So they went, and made the sepulcher sure,* <u>*sealing the stone*</u>, *and setting a watch." Matthew 27:65-66*

Pastor Don Anderson, one of the author's companions at the Garden Tomb. At the right is the iron rod that sealed Christ's tomb.

Iron and lead samples have been taken from the hole at the tomb proving that the Romans installed a steel pin set in rock with lead which was similar to Roman techniques used at other sites. The pin is still there, bent and sheared off as the angel rolled the huge stone away to openly display the empty tomb of the resurrected of Christ.

As Wyatt worked at the Garden Tomb site, he began to believe that Jeremiah hid the Ark of the Covenant in an underground cavern nearby. Wyatt believed that the hiding place for the Ark of the Covenant had once been accessed by a series of tunnels that originated in a huge underground cave known as Zedekiah's Cave which is under the city of

Jerusalem. You can visit the cave, also known as Solomon's Quarries. The entrance is located along the city wall just northeast of the Damascus Gate.

Zedekiah's Cave, photo by author

Wyatt believed that Jeremiah's hiding place for the Ark of the Covenant was located about 20 feet directly under the site of the crucifixion of Christ. He was convinced that an earthquake split the rocks and that the blood of Christ actually flowed down through a crack and was sprinkled upon the Mercy Seat in its hiding place.

This all sounds a little more than incredible, and perhaps unbelievable. Were it not for Wyatt's credibility in locating so many other historical sites, we would just pass his claims off as fantasy or wishful thinking.

We do know that the Biblical account of the crucifixion describes an incident that is in harmony with part of Wyatt's belief about the crack in the rocks –

"Jesus, when He had cried again with a loud voice, yielded up the spirit. And behold, the veil of the temple was torn in two from the top to the bottom; and the earth did quake, and <u>the rocks were rent</u> . . ." Matthew 27:50-51

One of the most remarkable finds of Ron Wyatt is now on display at the Israel Museum in Jerusalem. This tiny artifact alone adds credibility to his claims of something hidden in a cave below the Calvary Escarpment.

The Israel Museum claims that the Ivory Pomegranate is the only artifact ever found from Solomon's Temple. You can see the Ivory Pomegranate and even buy replica jewelry of it at the Israel Museum. Wyatt claimed that he brought the pomegranate out of his diggings below the crucifixion site and gave it to the former Director of the Jerusalem Antiquities. The point is that Wyatt found something below the Calvary Escarpment!

Is it possible that the blood of Christ actually dripped onto the Mercy Seat in literal fulfillment of *Leviticus 16:14* and the Old Testament type of the atoning sacrifice?

> *"And he* (the priest) *shall take of the blood of the bullock, and sprinkle it with his finger upon the mercy seat eastward; and before the mercy seat shall he sprinkle of the blood with his finger seven times."* Leviticus 16:14

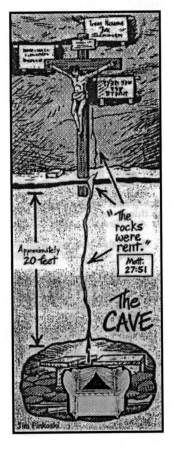

This possible literal fulfillment of the Old Testament picture of sacrifice and atonement would be an interesting and appealing theory; however, only time will tell about the accuracy of Wyatt's claims. God may bring such things to light as a testimony to His people Israel and the rest of the unbelieving world, or He may keep such things hidden if, in fact, that is how they occurred. We need to remember that the finished work of the Lord Jesus upon the cross does not demand the sprinkling of His blood on the physical Ark of the Covenant. Jesus' work is complete and satisfied the demands of the law so that sinners can be declared righteous by placing their faith in His atoning sacrifice upon the cross.

Wyatt died before he was able to confirm and prove his claims. At the time of this writing, the Wyatt Archeological Research, now led by Mr. Richard Rives, states emphatically that they have not been able to substantiate any of Wyatt's beliefs concerning the Ark of the Covenant despite continuing efforts and archeological explorations. A permit has apparently been granted to Wyatt Archeological Research by the Israel Antiquities Authority to fully excavate and open up the crucifixion site. It will be interesting to see if Wyatt's claims will ever be substantiated.

For the purposes of our study, if the Ark of the Covenant hidden in the days of Jerusalem's destruction is ever found and publicly revealed, you can be sure that zealous Jews will make every effort to move ahead in the rebuilding of the new Temple!

There is another possible event that could bring the entire Islamic world against the people of Israel, and that has to do with the future of the Dome of the Rock located on Mount Moriah (Temple Mount) in Jerusalem.

4.   DESTRUCTION OF THE DOME OF THE ROCK

Imagine the impact upon the Muslim world if someone were to sabotage the Dome of the Rock on Temple Mount. We can be assured that the State of Israel is making every effort to prevent Jewish extremists from harming this most sacred Muslim site. The destruction of the Dome of the Rock alone could ignite a world-wide Islamic holy war against modern-day Israel.

It is possible that the Dome of the Rock will be damaged, or even destroyed, by Islamic terrorists who would do anything to fuel hatred and create a crisis that would incite the Islamic world to become involved in a holy war against Israel and the United States. Destruction of the Dome of the Rock at the hands of Islamic extremists would have seemed impossible until the world witnessed the bombing of the Askariyah Mosque by Sunni militants on February 22, 2006. According to the Denver Post, Shiite mobs retaliated by attacking 27 Sunni mosques in Baghdad alone.

The destruction of the Dome of the Rock could take place at a moment's notice and would greatly accelerate the fulfillment of the events prophesied in the Scriptures.

Russia could take advantage of this fanatical religious hatred and lead the incensed "Holy Jihad" armies to invade the land that God calls "His Land." Russia's incentive would not be religious in nature nor would they have any interest in expelling Israelis from their land. However, a religious war could give great opportunity to Russia to seize control of the entire Persian Gulf area and thereby gain control over the economy of the world. Again, time will reveal how this all plays out.

MOTIVATED BY HATRED

The intense hatred of the Jewish people (and America) by the Islamic warriors who will one day invade Israel is fueled by centuries of religious animosity and desire to destroy all remembrances of their enemies and those who are not converted to Islam. The Palestinians and most of the Arab world will never be at rest until they control the entire city of Jerusalem, and every Israeli has been either expelled or executed. Add to that the possibility of a Temple rebuilding effort, and you have the perfect formula for a crazed and reckless army filled with enough hatred and wrath to attack Israel.

WHEN WILL THESE EVENTS OCCUR?

All of these events seem to be directly related to the prophesied destruction of the Russian-led Islamic army that invades the land of Israel from the north. The author is convinced that end-time Babylon will be attacked and destroyed at the same time.

No one knows when these events will occur, but a frenzied Islamic horde descending upon the mountains of Israel would be a definite clue of imminent things to come.

If you are interested in the development of end-time events, keep your eyes focused upon Israel and all the lands designated as God's land. Remember that all the land up to

---

the Euphrates River in Iraq are considered the land of God's people:

> *"In the same day the LORD made a covenant with Abram, saying, Unto thy seed have I given this land, <u>from the river of Egypt unto the great river, the river Euphrates</u>." Genesis 15:18*

Chapter 6
THE DESTRUCTION OF "END-TIME BABYLON"

Writing this chapter is not a pleasant task.

When I first began to seriously consider the Biblical prophecies of Babylon over twenty years ago, I became overwhelmed with a sense of foreboding and sorrow. I felt the same dismay when I first encountered the historic sites of Sodom and Gomorrah and began to visualize what had actually happened there.

The prospect that such a terrible scene of death and destruction will happen once again to an even larger end-time nation is almost too much to bear. Sometimes we have to pick up the ash and rub it between our fingers to get the full impact of a story we have all grown accustomed to.

So it is with the study of end-time Babylon and her tragic prophesied downfall. We may feel stunned and go through seasons of denial and disbelief. However, God presented the details that are before us for a reason, and we must not ignore that which He has made so clear.

It was no accident that the prophets wrote so vividly about the coming days of death and destruction. For some reason God wanted these things recorded in His Word as a warning and means of hope to those that will take His Word seriously.

As in the presentation of the Biblical description of Babylon in Chapter 3, we will attempt to present all of the passages that deal with the sudden demise of Babylon in the order in which they are presented in the Biblical texts of *Jeremiah chapters 50 and 51, Isaiah chapter 13* and *Revelation chapter 18.* We will also number the descriptive phrases for ease of future reference.

Jeremiah chapter 50

1.   THE LORD SPOKE AGAINST BABYLON

The destruction of end-time Babylon will come at the direct command of God. *"The Word that the LORD spoke against Babylon and against the land of the Chaldeans by Jeremiah the prophet . . ." (verse 1)*

It is interesting in this verse that God pronounced judgment upon Babylon AND the land of the Chaldeans. This may be an indication that His judgment will not only fall upon Babylon whom we have identified as a mighty end-time world power, the youngest of nations and center of commerce, but His judgment may also be directed to the *"land of the Chaldeans,"* the historic area of ancient Babylon. The prophets often wrote with local and distant implications just as they prophesied of contemporary and future events.

In addition to the destructive fires of God's wrath upon an immoral end-time civilization, God may put an end forever to any attempt to rebuild the historic city of Babylon which is located about fifty miles south of Baghdad, Iraq.

Jeremiah 50:18 re-enforces God's statement that He will be the One Who sends judgment against end-time Babylon. *"Behold, I will punish the king of Babylon and his land."* This verse makes it obvious that "Babylon" is part of a living society which has a political ruler and is more than the rebuilt site of the ancient and once proud city.

This day of destruction will be God's long overdue response to a society that has openly rejected His counsel and Word. In all honesty, it makes my heart tremble when decision after decision coming from our Federal Courts is against everything that remotely suggests there is a living God in Heaven. As I write, another decision has been handed down that denies a local school board in the state of Pennsylvania the right to even suggest that evolution is one of several theories.

2. SOUND THE ALARM

The message of Babylon's doom is to be published to the nations – *"Declare among the nations, and publish, and set up a standard; publish and conceal not; say Babylon is taken . . ." (verse 2)* There must be an urgency to warn the nation(s) of coming judgment. We are so prone to keep words of doom and gloom to ourselves, but the Lord of Light would have us warn others of impending darkness.

We do not have to be hateful in warning our nation of coming judgment by presenting the message of God's righteousness and coming wrath. In fact, if the message of the prophets does not break our hearts there is something terribly wrong with us. This is the emphasis of the psalmist – *"They that sow in tears shall reap in joy. He that goeth forth and weepeth, bearing precious seed, shall doubtless*

come again with rejoicing, bringing his sheaves with him."
Psalm 126:5-6

The entire message of this book is a heavy burden upon my heart, and I present it with tears for those who are not ready.

3. ATTACK FROM THE NORTH

The attack against end-time Babylon will come from the north. *"For out of the north there cometh up a nation against her, which shall make her land desolate, and none shall dwell in it; they shall remove themselves, they shall depart, both man and beast." Jeremiah 50:3*

Verse 9 of this chapter re-asserts the same thought – *"For lo, I will raise and cause to come up against Babylon an assembly of great nations from the north country . . ."*

It is interesting that *"Gog of the land of Magog"* (the king of Russia) has been described by the Prophet Ezekiel as coming *"from thy place out of the north parts, thou, and many peoples with thee." Ezekiel 38:15* If the United States is ever attacked with Russian strategic missiles they may come from all directions because of their massive submarine fleet armed with missiles and nuclear warheads. However, the direction of the attacking nation is to the north.

4. WHOLLY DESOLATE!

The attack from the north will devastate the land of Babylon. *"For out of the north there cometh up a nation against her, which shall make her land desolate." (verse 3)* The destruction is so thorough that any surviving men and animals will flee in utter panic. Most of us cannot even imagine such a dreadful day of calamity!

Verses 12 and 13 add to this descriptive fury – " . . . *the hindermost (youngest) of the nations shall be a wilderness, a dry land, and a desert. Because of the wrath of the LORD it shall not be inhabited, but it shall be wholly desolate . . .*"

What a horrific and graphic picture of total destruction – *"wholly desolate!"* Ground Zero at the devastated site of the Twin Towers was just that – *"wholly desolate."*

The Twin Towers were reduced to piles of smoldering debris--*"wholly desolate"!* Images of things to come?

5.   MISSILES RIGHT ON TARGET

The taking of Babylon sounds like a pre-empted missile attack as we learn from verse 9 – " . . . *from the north country . . . they shall set themselves in array; from there she shall be taken; their arrows shall be as of a mighty expert man; none shall return in vain."* Arrows (like missiles) are "launched" from one place to another. This is the picture the prophet is apparently painting for us.

The sudden attack from the north will be so effective that none of the *"arrows"* will miss their mark. There will be no deterring this massive air-strike as it descends suddenly from the north. God often uses one nation to bring judgment upon another. For example, the ungodly kingdom of ancient Babylon, under King Nebuchadnezzar, was used to bring chastening upon Jerusalem. The vile and cruel Assyrians were also used to disperse the ten tribes of northern Israel, just as God had warned.

6. THE DOOM OF RUSSIA'S ARMY

Ezekiel chapters 38 and *39* describe in detail the destruction of Gog of the land of Magog. God declared through Ezekiel, *"I am against thee, O Gog, the chief prince of Meshech and Tubal." Ezekiel 38:2*

When God destroys that far northern land He will apparently do it through modern day warfare – *"I will call for a sword against him throughout all my mountains, saith the LORD God; every man's sword against his brother." Ezekiel 38:21*

Supernatural destruction is also mentioned in this passage against the army of Gog as we read in *Ezekiel 38:22 – "And I will enter into judgment against him with pestilence and with blood; and I will rain upon him, and upon his hordes, and upon the many peoples that are with him, an <u>over-flowing rain, and great hailstones, fire, and brimstone.</u>"*

It would appear that Russia will be a leading partner of a huge military invasion of God's land, the land of Israel. God will intervene, and five out of six of the invading soldiers will perish, as we read in *Ezekiel 39:2 – "And I will turn thee back <u>and leave but the sixth part of thee,</u> and will cause thee to come up from the north parts, and will bring thee upon the mountains of Israel."*

7. THE DOOM OF RUSSIA'S HOMELAND

In addition to this *"overflowing rain of fire and brimstone"* God will *"send a fire on Magog <u>and among those who dwell securely in the coastlands."</u> Ezekiel 39:6*

Several events will take place, probably one right after the other, but possibly simultaneously:

1. The supernatural destruction of the huge army that invades Israel.
2. Fiery arrows will fall upon *"those dwelling in the coastlands."*
3. The sending of fire upon Magog, the homeland of Gog.

I believe that the Lord may be describing an all-out nuclear exchange between Magog and Babylon, and both will be left in smoldering ruins.

It should be remembered again that God's land, the land of Israel, includes much more than the area presently occupied by the present day State of Israel. God's promises to Abraham were an unconditional covenant. *"In the same day the LORD made a covenant with Abram, saying, Unto thy seed have I given this land, from the River of Egypt unto the great river, the river Euphrates . . ."* This is a description of almost the entire Middle East including all of present-day Israel, Lebanon, Syria, Saudi Arabia and Iraq. This is the land God gave to His people, and these lands have not been under the control of His Covenant Nation since the days of King David and Solomon.

But, these lands are designated God's just the same. The point is that the Russian army with its many allies may actually meet their doom somewhere east of present-day Israel. God mentions *"his mountains,"* so the horrendous rain of fire may fall on them east of the Jordan River as they attempt to come into modern-day Israel. Time will tell.

It is possible that the people of end-time Babylon will survive long enough to witness the beginning of the invasion of Israel from the north, perhaps even the destruction of Russia's huge Islamic army.

8. SHOCKING BEYOND BELIEF

The destruction of Babylon will shock the nations. *" . . . everyone that goeth by Babylon shall be appalled, and hiss at all her plagues . . ."* We are often shocked at televised images of death and destruction from natural disasters, but nothing will match the aftermath of these coming days of utter ruin!

The entire world will be stunned at the sudden devastation and aftermath of continuing death and suffering.

9.   THE SOUND OF BATTLE

The SOUND of battle – *"A sound of battle is in the land, and of great destruction."* *(verse 22)* How incredible that the prophets were given this kind of insight thousands of years before weapons of mass destruction were invented!

10.   THE EARTH IS MOVED

Whatever this sound is, it must be very great with awesome power, because we read in verse 46 – *"At the noise of the taking of Babylon the earth is moved, and the cry is heard among the nations."*

The weapons that the LORD calls against Babylon (and Magog) will be so great that the earth will literally be moved out of orbit. Can you imagine such destructive power? *Isaiah 13:13* adds to this terrible image of world-wide terror – *"I will shake the heavens, and the earth shall remove out of its place, in the wrath of the LORD of hosts, and in the day of His fierce anger."*

11.   MANY CITIES DESTROYED

According to the prophet, many cities will be destroyed during this time of international calamity. *Jeremiah 50:32* – *"And the most proud shall stumble and fall, and none shall raise him up; and I will kindle a fire in his cities, and it shall devour all round about him."* Who can deny that this sounds like the devastating power of nuclear warfare?

Add to this the words of *Jeremiah 51:43* – *"Her cities are a desolation, a dry land, and a wilderness, a land in which no man dwelleth, neither doth any son of man pass by it."*

12.   FORSAKEN LAND
Babylon will be left in ashes just like Sodom and Gomorrah as the prophet proclaimed. *"As God overthrew Sodom and Gomorrah, and their neighboring cities, saith the LORD, so shall no man abide there, neither shall any son of man dwell in her." Jeremiah 50:40* God declared that the destruction of end-time Babylon will be total and complete.

In the following verse Jeremiah described again from where this fury comes from — *"Behold, a people shall come from the north, and a great nation, and many kings shall be raised up from the borders of the earth. They shall hold the bow and the lance; they are cruel, and will not show mercy; their voice shall roar like the sea . . ." Jeremiah 50:41-42*

13.   PANIC
The knowledge that such an attack is forthcoming causes the leader of Babylon to panic as we read in *Jeremiah 50:43 -- "The king of Babylon hath heard the report of them, and his hands become feeble; anguish took hold of him, and pains as of a woman in travail."* Can you imagine the stress upon a leader who is aware of classified documentation of a forthcoming attack?

Jeremiah chapter 51

14.   DESTROYING WIND
Little more needs to be said. We already get the picture of total devastation, but God continues with the terrible

description of Babylon's day of judgment and utter destruction –

"Thus saith the LORD: Behold, I will raise up against Babylon, and against those who dwell in the midst of those who rise up against me, <u>a destroying wind.</u>" Jeremiah 51:1

We are all aware that one of the most destructive forces of a nuclear weapon is the incredible *"destroying wind."* Who can deny that this ancient description would appear to be modern-day weapons of warfare?

15.   SUDDEN DEVASTATION

The destruction of Babylon will come SUDDENLY, and there will be no time for protective measures. When the holocaust begins there will be no time to run and no place to hide. *Jeremiah 51:8 – "Babylon is <u>suddenly fallen</u> and destroyed."*

The New Testament book of Revelation reveals the same overwhelming truth:

". . . For in <u>one hour</u> is thy judgment come." *Revelation 18:10*

"For in <u>one hour</u> so great riches are come to nothing." Revelation 18:17

". . . for in <u>one hour</u> is she made desolate." Revelation 18:19

Before the advent of our weapons of mass destruction, such a claim of total destruction in one hour seemed totally impossible. In today's world we know that such devastation can happen in a moment's time.

Isaiah Chapter 13

The entire thirteenth chapter of Isaiah is given as another solemn warning to end-time Babylon. The Lord repeats His warnings time and time again so that some of us will take His words seriously and escape. There are no excuses for those who choose to ignore such clear warnings.

16.   FROM THE END OF HEAVEN

"They come from a far country, from the end of heaven, even the LORD, and the weapons of His indignation, to destroy the whole land." Isaiah 13:5

The sudden attack against Babylon will apparently come as an air-strike from a great distance, and the entire land will be totally destroyed.

17.   THE DAY OF THE LORD

The timing of this destructive judgment is detailed in *verse 6* where we read – *"Wail, for the DAY OF THE LORD is at hand; it shall come as a destruction from the Almighty."*

The message is repeated for emphasis in *verse 9 – "Behold, the DAY OF THE LORD cometh, cruel, both with wrath and fierce anger, to lay the land desolate; and He shall destroy the sinners out of it."*

According to the New Testament, the "Day of the LORD" will come suddenly and unannounced. *"For yourselves know perfectly that the DAY OF THE LORD so cometh as a thief in the night. For when they shall say, Peace and safety, then sudden destruction cometh upon them, as travail upon a woman with child, and they shall not escape."* 1 Thessalonians 5:2-3

Any woman who has ever given birth will tell you that the pains of birth come suddenly and without warning. In the middle of the night, often in the deepest of sleep, the pains begin, and there is no turning over and ignoring them. This is how God describes the "Day of the LORD." Much could be said about the "Day of the LORD" but one main observation is important in our study–The "Day of the LORD" is just the beginning of God's direct intervention once again into the affairs of man and the people of Israel. The "Day of the Lord" marks the beginning of the Tribulation, and it will come suddenly and unannounced. That *"day"* will commence with a terrible night of suffering and destruction for those who are not prepared and are left behind.

There is cause for great hope in the midst of all of this. We read in *1 Thessalonians 5:3 and 4 – " . . . and they shall not escape. But ye, brethren, are not in darkness, that that day should overtake you as a thief."* A few shall escape this day of wrath. We will attempt to further develop this hopeful thought in a later chapter.

18. DARKNESS AND NUCLEAR WINTER

Isaiah seemed to be describing a nuclear missile exchange and the aftermath of nuclear warfare. *"For the stars of heaven and the constellations thereof shall not give their light; the sun shall be darkened in its going forth, and the moon shall not cause its light to shine."* Isaiah 13:10

In the terrible aftermath of this nuclear nightmare, as multiple nuclear weapons are detonated, darkness and sub-zero nuclear winter will inflict additional suffering upon the survivors. After the initial destruction of heat and wind, other terrible and devastating effects of this kind of weapon continue to be felt for months. This type of weapon and its terrible results are described again in *Isaiah 47:14 – "Behold, they shall be like stubble; the fire shall burn them; they shall not deliver themselves from the power of the flame; there shall not be a coal to warm at, nor fire to sit before it."*

I believe this passage is graphically describing the effects of nuclear winter. Suddenly, when the atmosphere is destroyed by fire and the air becomes too thick to breathe, winter darkness descends upon those that escaped the initial blast and fire. The survivors of such a nightmare may be the greatest victims.

19.   THE UNFORTUNATE SURVIVORS

God is so explicit in His description of coming destruction that He gives us a picture of nuclear radiation and its misery. *"Therefore shall all hands be faint, and every man's heart shall melt; And they shall be afraid. Pangs and sorrows shall take hold of them; and they shall be in pain like a woman that travaileth.   They shall be amazed one at another; their faces shall be as flames."* Isaiah 13:7-8

Imagine the utter panic that will fall upon the world when an all-out nuclear exchange takes place. There are no words to describe such chaos and misery.

20.   RARE AS GOLD

Isaiah 13:12 tells us that man will become rare in the aftermath of the destruction of Babylon – *"I will make a man more rare than fine gold, even a man than the golden wedge of Ophir."*

When I was younger I spent some time dredging for gold in the streams of Colorado and California. I can assure you that gold is extremely rare and difficult to find. Even little nuggets hide themselves under rocks and sand in a gold pan, and only the discerning miner can find them. After the destruction of these mega-nations, man will become as rare as gold. It is hard to imagine such total devastation.

CONCLUSION

The reader is encouraged to read the entire chapters of *Jeremiah 50 and 51* in addition to *Isaiah, chapters 13 and 47* and *Revelation, chapter 18.*

God is not a sadistic tyrant anxiously awaiting the opportunity to cast misery upon mankind. He has expressed His love to all men by sending His Son, the Lord Jesus Christ, to pay the penalty of sin for us by dying on the cross. His offer to mankind is forgiveness, eternal life and hope to all that will believe on Him and trust Him as Savior and Lord.

But the solemn fact remains – *"The wages of sin is death . . ."* *Romans 6:23* Man's reckless disregard for God and His Word will one day lead to unbelievable suffering. For the most part, this suffering is really man-made. It is not the product of an evil and destructive tyrant as some mistakenly think the LORD to be.

The crystal-clear descriptions of Babylon and the warnings of coming destruction are written because God is a God of mercy. He desires that all men everywhere will repent and turn to Him for forgiveness and the promise of eternal life through faith in the Lord Jesus Christ. The only place of real peace and security in this desperate world is in the shelter of His wings.

Chapter 7
WORTHY OF DESTRUCTION?

Like the careful and deliberate strokes of an artist's brush, the prophets have painted a clear image of a great end-time nation referred to in Scripture as *"Babylon," "the daughter of Babylon"* and *"the glory of kingdoms."*

The portrait that emerges from a careful study of the words of the prophets is remarkably revealing but extremely dark and gloomy. This does not make for enjoyable reading, or writing for that matter. As the LORD directed each stroke of the prophetic artist's brush, an obvious image has been revealed, and whether we like the picture or not, we must not ignore its message.

GROWING ACCUSTOMED TO DARKNESS
We all face the danger of growing accustomed to the encroaching darkness of the world around us. Our spiritual eyes "adjust" and, in time, it doesn't seem all that dark. After a while the spiritual darkness into which our society has plummeted doesn't really seem so bad.

We ask ourselves, has America really become so immoral as to deserve total destruction from the hand of the righteous and holy God? Are we really so bad that we deserve judgment? What about the sins of the other nations? After all, we are not any worse than people in other places all over the globe.

There is one characteristic about America that makes it

stand out above all others: God has abundantly blessed our land and shed His Light upon us. No other nation on earth has been so cared for and enriched by the gracious hands of Divine Providence.

We have also enjoyed the light of God's Word, and its positive impact upon our society has been felt for over two hundred years. God has truly blessed us, and His truth has been our guiding light. The very concepts of liberty are derived from the teachings of Scripture.

But now we as a nation are turning away from God's Truth and embracing darkness.

All that's left to a once thriving community.

Turning away from truth makes us even more accountable as a nation than the ancient cities of Sodom and Gomorrah and the cities of the plain. They never had the light of the gospel of God's love and grace. They lived in moral darkness and never bathed in the glorious Light of God's Word.

Jesus lamented over the hardness of hearts of three cities in ancient Israel. Those cities were built along the shores of the Sea of Galilee.

The ruins of ancient Chorazin.

Jesus visited the communities often. He taught the people and displayed His love and power as He healed their bodies and miraculously fed them from a few fish and loaves. *Matthew 11:20-23* reveals -

"Then began He to upbraid the cities in which most of His mighty works were done, because they repented not: Woe unto thee, Chorazin! Woe unto thee, Bethsaida!

For if the mighty works, which were done in you, had been done in Tyre and Sidon, they would have repented long ago in sackcloth and ashes . . . *And thou, Capernaum, which art exalted unto heaven, shalt be brought down to hell; for if the mighty works, which have been done in thee, had been done in Sodom, it would have remained until this day.* "

You can visit the sites of Capernaum and Chorazin. They are located right along the Sea of Galilee, but nothing remains more than piles of rocks and debris. They have never been rebuilt, just as Jesus said when He pronounced their coming doom.

We cannot even find most of the remains of ancient Bethsaida. Some believe it was built along the northernmost part of the Sea of Galilee, but even the ruins appear to have been removed.

Several miles north of the Sea of Galilee are the ruins of another city called Gamla. This was the fortress built atop a camel-like mountain by a large group of "zealots" who defied Rome. They resisted the taxes and authority of their Roman enemies until they were eventually attacked by the Roman Legions after the destruction of Jerusalem in 70 A.D. Rather than submit to the brutalities of their conqueror, over 5,000 men, women and children leaped off the southern cliffs of the city to their death. Their resistance was very similar to that of the defenders of Masada who also chose to end their lives rather than submit or give a victory to their oppressors.

It is possible that many of the rocks used to build the

fortress at Gamla may have come from Bethsaida. The point being that the coming judgment that Jesus pronounced upon the cities that rejected His Word, was thorough and complete. None of the cities have ever been rebuilt.

WHAT MARKED THEM FOR JUDGMENT?
Jesus made it very clear –

> ". . . for if the mighty works, which have been done in thee, had been done in Sodom, it would have remained to this day." Matthew 11:23

Imagine that! Jesus said if the people of Sodom had seen the things that these cities had seen, they would have repented and lived!

God had given the communities along the Sea of Galilee the light of His Son. Jesus taught the people and revealed the glory of His Heavenly Father. People that have the light and reject it are accountable.

America is accountable. The present darkness smothering our land is the deliberate choice of the people, and that encroaching darkness will eventually lead to our doom. Nobody likes that message, but it must be proclaimed!

What an incredible tragedy to have the truth and light, yet deliberately walk in darkness!

God has spoken in words that we can easily understand –

> "Righteousness exalteth a nation, but sin is a reproach to any people." Proverbs 14:34

"Ye adulterers and adulteresses, know ye not that the friendship of the world is enmity with God? Whosoever, therefore, will be a friend of the world is the enemy of God." James 4:4

"Blessed is the nation whose God is the LORD; and the people whom He hath chosen for His own inheritance." Psalm 32:12

Like a mathematical formula, there is a reverse or contrasting truth to that verse in *Psalms*. The contrast implied is <u>cursed</u> is the nation who has rejected the LORD. *"Blessed is the nation whose God is the LORD," but* <u>cursed is the nation who rejects the LORD</u>!

DESERVING OF JUDGMENT?
Is America really deserving of God's judgment? Perhaps not from our distorted viewpoint, but definitely from the viewpoint of the God Who is totally holy, just and right.

The fact is, when men turn away from the light of God's truth, there is nothing left but the darkness of eternal destruction. The *"wages of sin is death." Romans 6:23* There is no other option: light and life or darkness and death! What will America choose in years to come?

Even the cruel and ruthless nation of the Assyrians was given the opportunity to repent and turn away from their wicked ways. The Prophet Jonah reluctantly entered into the capital city of the Assyrians and declared that God's day of justice was coming and that the city of Nineveh would be destroyed. (Actually, Jonah was dragged into Nineveh by

God, kicking and screaming all the way!)

The pagan king repented in sackcloth and ashes and declared a total fast of all food and water for all the people, and even for their animals. Judgment was withheld for over 100 years, illustrating the fact that God is, indeed, a God of mercy and grace. *"And God saw their works, that they turned from their evil way; and God repented of the evil that He had said that He would do unto them, and He did it not."* *Jonah 3:10*

God's heart of mercy and grace was wonderfully revealed to Jonah who was disgusted that God had not destroyed the merciless enemies of Israel. God said to His angry prophet – *"And should not I spare Nineveh, that great city, in which are more than six score thousand persons that cannot discern between their right hand and their left hand; and also much cattle?" Jonah 4:11*

GOD BLESS AMERICA!
We that believe in the Lord Jesus Christ need to fervently pray that God would grant unto us and our fellow Americans, a spirit of genuine repentance, so that His judgment might somehow be delayed.

The day of Babylon's destruction is coming. That cannot be avoided. The prophets spoke clearly and distinctly. But, perhaps that day can be delayed through the prayer and repentance of a nation marked for God's eventual justice.

GROWING ACCUSTOMED
My youngest son, Chris, built a lovely home in eastern Ohio

several years ago. They live in a pleasant community east of Cleveland where he pastors a young and growing church. The homes and yards in the community are attractive to the eye. Anyone would be happy to live in such pleasant surroundings.

When the house was ready to be painted, my wife and I spent a week with them to help them finish up so they could move in.

We borrowed several buckets of water from a neighbor to clean up the airless paint sprayer and brushes. I was so repulsed by the terrible smell of the water that I didn't even want to put my hands into it. Every well in the area has the stench of sulfur. The water has been tested and retested and is perfectly safe for drinking, but the smell is terrible.

In the process of time, we all become accustomed to our surroundings. When we visit them now we find that the water doesn't seem to smell nearly as bad as it had on that first whiff. What has changed? Not the water, but our response to it. After several trips to Ohio I can even brush my teeth in it and not feel nearly so defiled. My son's family doesn't even smell its offensive odor any more!

So it is with the moral stench that fills our noses in our beloved land. After a while we are prone to say, "It's not all that bad."

A STENCH IN GOD'S NOSE

The fact of the matter is, we have all become desensitized to that which is a total and terrible stench in the nostrils of our Holy God.

"I have spread out my hands all the day unto a rebellious people, that walketh in a way that was not good, after their own thoughts; A people that provoketh me to anger continually to my face . . . these are a smoke in my nose, a fire that burneth all the day." Isaiah 65:2- 3, 5

When I was a youngster growing up in the quaint village of Lamont, Michigan, everyone burned their garbage in a barrel "out back." We were always very careful to check the wind direction before lighting those detestable fires, so the breeze would take the smoke away from our own house, and toward the neighbors.

Of course, the neighbors waited until the wind was blowing the other way before they got even and polluted our air. As the popular saying declares, "What goes around comes around!"

Like the stench of burning garbage, the smoke of our decaying and immoral society has reached the holy nostrils of the God of heaven. His justice will eventually fall upon the nation that has had the light and now chooses darkness.

IS THERE ANY HOPE?

Is it possible to escape the stroke of God's wrath upon a nation? Is there any hope in the midst of such gloom and darkness of coming judgment?

The answer is a resounding "YES," but you may be surprised where that hope is found.

Chapter 8
A FEW SHALL ESCAPE!

We have discovered that the ancient prophets of God painted a depressingly gloomy picture of death and destruction. Several large end-time nations will experience the judgment and wrath of God as He removes His restraining power from the hearts of sinful men and they begin to hurl their weapons of mass destruction at one another.

One of those nations, without dispute, is the northern kingdom of Russia who will invade the lands of Israel with a gigantic army of Islamic soldiers *(Ezekiel 38:1-6.)* The other nation apparently involved in the terrible melee is called the *"daughter of Babylon"* and *"the glory of kingdoms."*

"Babylon," the great end-time nation, is described as the youngest, most wealthy and powerful nation that ever existed. She is a nation born from a motherland and is a melting pot of all nationalities.

It would appear that God may be describing the land that many of us love, the United States of America. No other nation on earth so perfectly fits all of the descriptions found in the Scriptures (see Chapter 3). If it were another nation from another time, or if the prophecies had already been fulfilled, we would all be relieved. However, the word pictures of the prophets are remarkably descriptive of modern-day America.

Our presentation of this material is not meant to alarm or depress, but to warn. Hopefully, the things described can be delayed through a national awakening and repentance.

THERE IS GOOD NEWS
There were a few fortunate people who were delivered from the fiery destruction of Sodom. Lot and his two daughters escaped because of the direct intervention of God.

Just as a few escaped the downpour of burning sulfur of Sodom's judgment, so a few can confidently expect to be evacuated before the fires fall upon the unsuspecting end-time nations.

Let's take another look at Sodom and Gomorrah and see how this confidence of deliverance can become ours.

"As it was in the days of Lot; they did eat, they drank, they bought, they sold, they planted, they built; But <u>the same day that Lot went out of Sodom, it rained fire and brimstone from heaven, and destroyed them all.</u>" Luke17:28-29

LOT WAS NOT A PERFECT, GOD-FEARING MAN
Far from it! He had subjected his entire household to the influences of an immoral and corrupt society. We learn from *Genesis 13:10-11* that he chose to lead his clan to the *"plain of Jordan"* because it was *"well watered everywhere before the LORD destroyed Sodom and Gomorrah."*

Any man seeking the welfare of his family would have chosen a bountiful land that would sustain their herds. But

Lot *"pitched his tent toward Sodom,"* perhaps to be close to the markets where he could buy and sell. The conveniences of the city would be appealing to any man and his family.

The next downward step for Lot was to be in Sodom. And soon Sodom was in the hearts and lives of most of the family that he loved. Obviously, the love of Sodom caused Lot's wife to look back (perhaps longingly). She was probably destroyed in an area that today is a massive salt deposit.

Lot's sons-in-law and hired workers apparently embraced the wicked lifestyle of the Sodomites. When Lot was told by the angels that destruction was imminent, he went out to warn his family –

> *"And Lot went out, and spoke unto his sons-in-law, who married his daughters, and said, Up, get you out of this place; for the LORD will destroy this city. But he seemed as one that mocked unto his sons-in-law."* *Genesis 19:14*

The men who had married Lot's daughters thought that their father-in-law had lost his mind. Was he drunk? What was wrong with this man? And then, they all perished in the blazing inferno.

You may feel the same way as you read an expose' like this. God would surely never condemn a great place like America! Anyone who would even suggest such calamity for a modern nation as great as the United States must have lost some of his marbles. He must be "playing with half a deck!" Maybe his batteries are running low!

Lot led his family into harm's way. What an epitaph for a man who had experienced the redeeming grace of God.

BUT LOT WAS STILL A GOD-FEARING MAN
Lot was NOT PERFECT, but Lot was forgiven. The testimony of Scripture is that Lot was declared righteous by God. This is hard to understand because Lot didn't live righteously. Lot was certainly a poor testimony of one who believed in God.

God turned the cities of Sodom and Gomorrah into ashes and made them an example to the rest of the world. But God – "... *delivered just LOT, vexed with the filthy manner of life of the wicked (for that righteous man dwelling among them, in seeing and hearing, vexed his righteous soul from day to day with their unlawful deeds)."* 2 Peter 2:7-8

There are two important truths that we can learn from the Scriptures regarding this *"just man"* whose name was Lot:

1. GOD DELIVERED THE RIGHTEOUS, BEFORE HE DESTROYED THE UNRIGHTEOUS
Lot's deliverance from Sodom before the blazing fireballs fell is a pattern that was first seen in a previous episode in the Bible. The first example of God's deliverance before destruction was demonstrated in the days of Noah.

"And as it was in the days of Noah, so shall it be also in the day of the Son of man. They did eat, they drank, they married wives, they were given in marriage, until the day that Noah entered into the ark and the flood came,

and destroyed them all." Luke 17:26-28

What happened during the days of the flood will be repeated
again in the future. After Noah and his family were
DELIVERED into the ark, the floods came and
DESTROYED the ungodly. The same pattern can be
observed with Lot and his two daughters who were believers
in Jehovah. As soon as the angels had delivered them from
the city of Sodom, the brimstone began to fall and totally
destroyed the entire godless society. The New Testament
Scriptures tell us that deliverance is the direct act of God.

> *"The Lord knoweth how to deliver the godly out of*
> *temptations, and to reserve the unjust unto the day of*
> *judgment to be punished." 2 Peter 2:9*

I am convinced that this Biblical pattern of deliverance of
the godly before the destruction of the ungodly will be
repeated when *"the daughter of Babylon"* is destroyed.
Isaiah chapter 13 relates the fall of Babylon with the *"Day*
of the LORD."

> *"Wail; for the Day of the LORD is at hand; it shall*
> *come as a destruction from the Almighty . . . and*
> *Babylon, the glory of kingdoms . . . shall be as when*
> *God overthrew Sodom and Gomorrah." Isaiah 13:6*
> *and 19*

The *"Day of the LORD"* is the time when God will once
again intervene directly into the affairs of His people, the
nation of Israel. This is the topic found throughout the
prophecy of Joel. The *"Day of the LORD"* is not just a

twenty-four hour day, but the entire period of time describing God's work of bringing His covenant people to repentance and renewal.

> *"Alas for the day! For the day of the LORD is at hand, and as a destruction from the Almighty shall it come."*
> *Joel 1:15*

> *"Blow the trumpet in Zion, and sound an alarm in my holy mountain. Let all the inhabitants of the land tremble; for the day of the LORD cometh, for it is near at hand; A day of darkness and of gloominess, a day of clouds and of thick darkness . . . a fire devoureth before them, and behind them a flame burneth . . ."*
> *Joel 2:1-3*

The New Testament reaffirms that the Day of the LORD will come suddenly as a day of great destruction. *"For yourselves know perfectly that the Day of the LORD so cometh as a thief in the night. For when they shall say peace and safety, then sudden destruction cometh upon them, as travail upon a woman with child, and they shall not escape." 1 Thessalonians 5:2-3*

In the midst of such overwhelming calamity, God says – *"Blow the trumpet . . . sound an alarm . . ."* There is deliverance for those who will heed the warning.

NOT JUST WISHFUL THINKING
The LORD made it very clear in *1 Thessalonians 5:3* that *"darkness shall come upon <u>them</u>"* and that *"<u>they</u> shall not escape."* But there are some that will be delivered.

"But ye, brethren, are not in darkness that that day should overtake you as a thief." (verse 4)

"They" (the unbelievers) shall be overcome with darkness and destruction, but *"ye"* (believers) will be delivered. The book of *First Thessalonians* was written to believers in the Lord Jesus Christ in order to alleviate their fears that they had been left behind and would suffer the trials of the Day of the Lord.

What a great encouragement this is to every person who has placed his or her faith in the Lord Jesus Christ! This is the same *"hope"* that is referred to in *Chapter 4* of the same epistle of *First Thessalonians* –

"But I would not have you to be ignorant, brethren, concerning them who are asleep, that ye sorrow not, even as others who have no hope. For if we believe that Jesus died and rose again, even so them also who sleep in Jesus will God bring with Him. For this we say unto you by the Word of the Lord, that we who are alive and remain until the coming of the Lord, shall not precede them who are asleep. For the Lord Himself shall descend from heaven with a shout, and with the trump of God; and the dead in Christ shall rise first; Then we who are alive and remain shall be caught up together with them in the clouds, to meet the Lord in the air; and so shall we ever be with the Lord. Wherefore, comfort one another with these words."   *1 Thessalonians 4:13-18*

The Day of the LORD is not just a day of destruction. It will also be a day of deliverance. The coming of the Lord

Jesus Christ in the air to deliver His blood-bought people from this sinful earth is one of the foundation stones of Biblical Christianity. The Lord is coming to DELIVER His people. He reinforces that truth in *1 Thessalonians 5:9 – "For God hath not appointed us to wrath but to obtain salvation by our Lord Jesus Christ."*

Following the Biblical pattern as seen in the days of Noah and Lot, after God delivers those who trust Him and know Him, the fires of destruction will fall.

There is another truth we need to learn from Lot:

2.   GOD   DELIVERED   THE   <u>RIGHTEOUS</u>, BEFORE HE DESTROYED THE <u>UNRIGHTEOUS</u>

The statement above is identical to that made in Point #1, but notice the difference in emphasis. Lot shouldn't have been in Sodom in the first place, but the Bible calls him a <u>righteous</u> man. He had placed his faith in God and it was accounted unto him for righteousness. Lot was righteous, not because he lived righteously, but because he had placed his faith in the LORD of Righteousness.

Lot is a picture of a righteous man living in an unrighteous society. We don't believe that Lot was a partaker of all the evil around him, because Scripture claims that the ungodliness tormented his soul – *"For that righteous man dwelling among them, in seeing and hearing, vexed his righteous soul from day to day with their unlawful deeds." 2 Peter 2:8*

LUKEWARM FAITH

In the *Book of Revelation*, the last book of the Bible, there is the description of seven churches in chapters two and three. Those seven churches were messages sent from the Lord Jesus Christ through the hand of the Apostle John as he lived in exile on the Isle of Patmos. Each of the seven letters that were delivered to the churches had the following applications:

a) PRIMARY ASSOCIATION   That is, the letters were written to those local congregations with a specific message from the Lord.

b) PERSONAL APPLICATION   Each letter speaks to us individually today just as it spoke to the churches two thousand years ago.

c) PROPHETIC ANTICIPATION   Each letter outlined a specific period of time in the history of the church.

Laodicea was the last of the seven churches, thus the message was to "Christendom" as it will be during the last days. The Lord called the believers at Laodicea *"lukewarm."* They were neither hot nor cold even though they thought they were wealthy and in need of nothing.

Sadly, the church of Laodicea is a picture of the church in today's world. Self-sufficient. Satisfied. Filled with pride. But terribly bankrupt.

The end-of–the–age church is a reflection of Lot who lived in the days of Sodom. Sad to say, many men declared righteous by faith in Christ still live unrighteously in our godless society.

WALKING THE TALK OR JUST TALKING THE WALK?

Perhaps you have placed your faith in the Lord Jesus Christ and received His gift of eternal life. How does your life measure up? Are you "walking the talk" or just "talking the walk?"

Lot was a shameful picture of many believers who refuse to separate themselves from ungodliness. Some people may be genuine in the area of faith and doctrine, but not Christ-honoring in their daily conduct and lives.

Even though Lot was living in the wicked city of Sodom and was possibly a community leader or even a judge (he *"sat in the gate of Sodom"*), he was declared righteous by the LORD. The Bible says that God *". . . delivered just LOT, vexed with the filthy manner of life of the wicked (for that righteous man dwelling among them, in seeing and hearing, vexed his righteous soul from day to day with their unlawful deeds)." 2 Peter 2:7-8*

HOW DOES A MAN BECOME RIGHTEOUS BEFORE GOD?

Sadly, there is much confusion about this topic in today's world. Most believe that righteousness is a result of religious commitment and considerable personal effort. This is not God's way as taught clearly throughout the Scriptures. The "social gospel" has permeated most of the main-line denominations which once proclaimed the gospel of salvation by faith.

The religion of man is basically one of self-effort. Many confused groups teach that "character determines destiny." Most people believe that if you are good enough, you will be weighed in the balances and granted access to eternal life by your good works.

Nothing could be further from the truth. Character does not determine eternal destiny. Conversion determines destiny! Jesus said – *"Ye must be born-again."* *John 3:3* Spiritual rebirth is God's miracle of conversion whereby genuine believers in Christ are forgiven and transformed by God's Holy Spirit abiding in their lives.

The fact is, if man could attain righteousness by his own self-effort, he would have plenty to boast about. Imagine heaven filled with people prancing around in pride, boasting of their own goodness and righteousness! That is not what heaven is going to be all about. God detests a proud and boastful spirit. He tells us clearly that good works have nothing to do with salvation. *"For by grace are ye saved through faith, and that not of yourselves, it is the gift of God, not of works, lest any man should boast."* *Ephesians 2:8-9*

UNDESERVED MERIT: THE GIFT OF GOD

"Grace" is the undeserved favor of God. By grace, God gives us what we do not deserve.

Mercy is also an undeserved gift from God. By God's mercy, He does not give us what we do deserve, namely judgment.

Forgiveness and eternal life are free gifts from God given to all that will simply come to Him by faith. You may ask, "Faith in what?" The object of our faith is vital.

Remember the sons of Adam? Cain had faith in the fruits of his own efforts. He brought the very best that he could produce. But his gifts were not accepted by God.

Abel brought the sacrifice of an innocent lamb. His faith was in the God of mercy who would accept the blood sacrifice of the lamb in his place. His sacrifice was acceptable to God.

The two brothers illustrate the vast difference between the "religion of man" (Cain) and "redemption" which is of God. The brothers were both taught the same message, but their responses were very different.

THE INNOCENT DIES FOR THE GUILTY

Throughout the Scriptures, God used the sacrifices of innocent animals to illustrate and emphasize several important truths:

1. The death of an innocent animal in the place of the sinner was a terrible thing to witness. Death is never pleasant. Imagine watching the helpless animal die because of your iniquities. I'm sure that Adam and Eve were shocked and grieved when the LORD Himself slew the first animal to ever die to make coverings for them. They had never seen death before, and now they witnessed the shedding of blood because of their sinful disobedience.

God warned Adam that there were dire consequences

to sin – *"But of the tree of the knowledge of good and evil, thou shalt not eat of it; for in the day that thou eatest thereof, thou shalt surely die."* Genesis 2:17

The death that man experienced was threefold:

a) Man was immediately separated from fellowship with God. He no longer thought like God thought, and his sin became a terrible barrier between him and his Creator – *"But your iniquities have separated between you and your God, and your sins have hidden His face from you, that He will not hear."* Isaiah 59:2

We often refer to this broken fellowship with God as <u>spiritual death</u>. Adam and Eve died spiritually the moment they disobeyed.

b) Man <u>began to die physically</u>. He was created by God to live in eternal fellowship with his Creator. But now physical death would be the experience of every man.

c) The ultimate curse of death is <u>eternal death</u>, or separation from God forever. None of us can even imagine what it would be like to live eternally, consciously miserable and separated from the God of life and light.

Jesus spoke frequently about Hell. In fact, He spoke more about Hell than He did about Heaven.

Understand this: the raging fires of Hell are worse

than any fire imagined by man. The fiery brimstone that rained upon Sodom and Gomorrah was nothing in comparison to the anguish of living eternally apart from the God of love, joy, peace, light and life. Imagine living in a total vacuum completely devoid of God. God is love. In this vacuum you would exist with absolutely no love. God is light. In the vacuum of eternal Hell you would live in total darkness.

Death, in all of its hideous forms, was passed on from generation to generation. What an incredible blight and curse upon mankind. *"Wherefore, as by one man sin entered into the world, and death by sin, and so death passed upon all men, for all have sinned." Romans 5:12*

Later, after Adam and Eve were expelled from the Garden of Eden because of their rebellion and disobedience, they would be overwhelmed in grief as their sinful natures were passed down upon their children, and Cain would murder his brother Abel.

The death of the innocent animals taught man just how terrible sin is, but there was another valuable lesson.

2. When a person would bring his sacrifice to the priest, he would place his hand upon the head of the animal and confess his transgressions. The animal would die as his substitute. The Bible teaches that there is no forgiveness apart from the shedding of blood – *"And almost all things are by the law purged with blood, and without the shedding of blood there is no remission." Hebrews 9:22*

The blood sacrifices of the Old Testament all pointed to one event, the sacrifice of the Perfect Lamb of God upon the cross in payment for the sins of all men, past, present and future. Jesus Christ, the virgin-born Son of God, came to this earth to die as a sin-substitute for all men. What an incredible thing that God, Himself, would offer Himself as the sacrifice for our sins. What kind of love would cause the Eternal Creator to become man and die in order to save us from the eternal ravages of Hell and separation from God?

FAITH ALONE IN CHRIST ALONE

When we believe in the finished work of Jesus Christ upon that cross and invite Him to be our Savior and Lord, we are given the gift of God which is eternal life. How can this be? How can it be so simple?

A remarkable thing occurred on the cross as Jesus was dying in our place. He was bearing the sins of the world, as Isaiah said – *"But He was wounded for our transgressions, He was bruised for our iniquities; the chastisement for our peace was upon Him, and with His stripes we are healed."* *Isaiah 53:5* The Savior died, not as a martyr or victim of Roman brutality, but He died willingly, lovingly, in our place!

Isaiah continued – *"All we like sheep have gone astray; we have turned everyone to his own way, and the LORD hath laid on Him, the iniquity of us all."* *Isaiah 53:6*

TRANSFERENCE

Not only were our sins all transferred to the Lord Jesus Christ as He hung upon that Roman cross, but something else remarkable happens when we place our complete faith in what He did for us. His righteousness is transferred to us. Isaiah foresaw that wonderful truth when he declared –

"I will greatly rejoice in the LORD, my soul shall be joyful in my God; for He hath clothed me with the garments of salvation, He hath covered me with the robe of righteousness, as a bridegroom decketh himself with ornaments, and as a bride adorneth herself with her jewels." Isaiah 61:10

Covered over with a robe of righteousness: that is salvation based entirely on what God did for us! There is no human merit involved. There will be no boasting among the recipients of God's grace. Genuine praise and thanksgiving will flow from the hearts of those who are redeemed.

The Lord's mercy is truly beyond human comprehension!

His mercy is also beyond human compensation, because we cannot pay for it. His mercy, grace and the gift of eternal life are all free. Not cheap, but free! The death of the Son of God was the highest price that God could possibly pay, so that we who trust Him and receive Him as Savior and Lord, can enjoy the gifts of His grace for eternity.

All of this is available to anyone who will call upon Him in simple faith. *"That if thou shalt confess with thy mouth the Lord Jesus, and shalt believe in thine heart that God hath raised Him from the dead, thou shalt be saved. For with the heart man believeth unto righteousness; and with the mouth confession is made unto salvation. For the scripture saith, Whosoever believeth on Him shall not be ashamed . . .*

for whosoever shall call upon the Name of the Lord shall be saved." Romans 10:9-10, 13

What grace! What mercy! What love!

No wonder Isaiah could plead with the nation of Israel to repent and return to the LORD. With a broken heart, he cried out – *"Come now, and let us reason together, saith the LORD, though your sins be as scarlet, they shall be as white as snow; though they be red like crimson, they shall be as wool." Isaiah 1:18*

ONLY ONE SIN CONDEMNS MANKIND
There is no sin that God cannot cleanse and forgive except the sin of unbelief.

The worst criminal can receive the grace of God by simply believing in the Lord Jesus Christ and turning away from sin to the Savior.

It was reported that mass murderer, Ted Bundy, received the Lord Jesus as his personal Savior before he was executed in Florida for his many grisly crimes. God's grace and mercy knows no limit . . . except unbelief.

Won't you trust Him today and be born into His eternal family?

"But as many as received Him, to them gave he the power to become the children of God, even to them that believe on His Name." John 1:12

In light of the uncertainty of life and the horrendous events prophesied to fall upon this earth, RUN! Run to the Savior, the Lord Jesus Christ. He waits for you with open arms of forgiveness and grace!

Chapter 9
END-TIMES SCENARIO

Speculations about the sequence of future events swirl as men try to guess what is going to happen in the future. God gave us His Word so that we don't have to live by mere speculation.

As time goes by, we understand more and more of what the prophets wrote in light of current events and the fulfillment of the prophetic scriptures. As we mentioned earlier, it is always easier to properly interpret the prophetic scriptures after they have come to pass.

The challenge is to objectively consider all the words of the prophets and maintain an open mind and teachable spirit.

What I want to share in this brief chapter is my own personal conclusions after years of study and observation.

In an attempt to be objective and let the Scriptures speak for themselves, let's begin by listing some things that we KNOW for certain:

1. During what the Bible calls "end-times" or "last days" (*Daniel 8:17; 11:40; 12:4, 9; and 2 Timothy 3:1*), the people of Israel will return to their God-given land. (*Ezekiel 36:24-28, Ezekiel chapter 37*)

2. Someday there will be an invasion of Israel from the north, and God will supernaturally intervene to protect His people in His Land. Russia, with hordes of hateful Islamic warriors, will descend upon the mountains of Israel. Five out of six of their invading forces will be killed as they suddenly turn their swords upon one another in deadly confusion and chaos. *(Ezekiel chapter 38)*

3. It will take the people of Israel seven months to bury their dead enemies who will be buried east of the Dead Sea in the mountain valleys of present-day Jordan. The burial ground will be called The Valley of Hamon-gog which means "the multitude of Gog." *(Ezekiel 39:11-14)*

4. God will call for fire upon both Magog (the Russian homeland) and among those who live in the coastlands (beyond the seas). *(Ezekiel 39:1-6)*

5. An end-time nation referred to as *"Babylon"* or *"the daughter of Babylon"* will be suddenly attacked from the north and left in total ruins. The center of world commerce will have been destroyed, and the merchants of the earth shall weep as they stand afar off for the fear of her burning. *(Jeremiah, chapters 50 and 51; Isaiah, chapter 13; Revelation, chapter 18)*

6. Sometime during all of these horrific events, God will quietly cause every born-again believer in the Lord Jesus Christ to suddenly and mysteriously disappear, just as He caused Lot and his daughters to be delivered before the destruction of Sodom. *(1 Thessalonians*

4:13-18; 1 Thessalonians 5:1-9; Luke 17:26-29)

7. The false messiah will convince the world that he, and he alone, can bring lasting world peace, and through great words of deception he will be given world-wide authority. *(Revelation 6:1-8; Revelation, chapter 13)*

8. The false messiah and deceiver, referred to as the man of sin or the "anti-Christ," will confirm a covenant with Israel for seven years, allowing them to rebuild their Temple. He will promise them safety and peace in the land that God gave them through their national fathers, Abraham, Isaac and Jacob. *(Daniel 9:24-27; Revelation, chapters 6 and 13)*

9. The false messiah, as supreme world ruler, shall break his covenant with Israel after three and a half years and shall enter into their newly built temple and desecrate the Holy Place. This despicable act is referred to as the *"abomination that makes all things desolate."* *(Daniel 9:27 and Matthew 24:15)* He will declare open warfare upon the people of Israel and the "Tribulation saints" who refuse the "mark of the beast," which is apparently an implanted identification chip placed in either the right hand or forehead. He will seek to exterminate both Jews and the Tribulation believers in Messiah Jesus as he declares himself to be God and demands universal worship. *(Daniel 9:27; 11:36-44; Revelation, chapter 13)*

10. The people of Israel will flee from their land and seek refuge in the deserts and mountains of Israel. Many will find safety in Petra, the ancient stone city of

the Edomites. *(Psalm 60:10-11)*

11. The *"sign of the Son of Man in heaven"* shall appear as the *"King of kings"* descends upon earth in power and great glory with a heavenly army. *(Matthew 24:27, 29-30; Revelation 19:11-16)* During this time, the armies of earth will assemble in the Valley of Megiddo to do battle against the coming LORD of Hosts.

12. The True Messiah of Israel will return to the earth and destroy His enemies with the sword of His Word. He will descend upon the Mount of Olives and establish a kingdom of real peace and prosperity. *(Zechariah, chapter 14; Ezekiel, chapter 47)*

This list is not all inclusive, of course, but contains the major events that will transpire at the beginning and during the seven-year period of time known as the Tribulation or *"Time of Jacob's Trouble."* We will try to weave these events together in a brief possible scenario that includes all of the prophetic events.

RETURN TO THE LAND!

From all over the world incredible numbers of the people of Israel begin to return to the land promised to Abraham. The State of Israel continues to struggle with hateful terrorists and avowed enemies who are determined to exterminate every Jew and take control of the whole land.

Increased terrorism worldwide and rumors of weapons of mass destruction in the hands of deadly extremists cause even more people in America to panic and migrate to Israel and other nations where they hope to find safety.

FOUND AT LAST!
Suddenly the world is abuzz about an incredible discovery in Israel. It is reported that the long lost Ark of the Covenant has been located and is being brought back into the city of Jerusalem. Jewish people are excited about the prospect of building a new Temple on Temple Mount in Jerusalem where Solomon's Temple once stood. Religious leaders totally denounce the report that the blood of Jesus Christ had sprinkled on the Mercy Seat at the time of His crucifixion, and the priests feverously prepare to re-establish and initiate the ancient animal sacrificial system.

DOWN WITH THE DOME!
Something catastrophic happens to the Dome of the Rock. No one knows who is responsible for sure, but the Islamic world is furious. The possibility of a bomb being planted by Islamic terrorists is rumored, but the State of Israel is blamed.

INVASION FROM THE NORTH!

Millions of fanatical Moslem warriors from many countries begin massing to the north and east of Israel. Russia, along with the cooperation of many other nations, intervenes by sending a huge contingency into the Middle East, possibly as United Nations appointed "peacekeepers." Their ultimate and secret purpose is to seize control of the entire Persian Gulf area and thereby control the economy of the entire world.

As the huge army begins to cross the Jordan River, just east of Jerusalem, an incredible thing happens. The invading soldiers suddenly turn their weapons upon one another in confusion. Death and devastation are everywhere!

Only one out of six of the Russian soldiers survives in the worst slaughter and shedding of blood in modern-day history.

Without any warning, Russia suddenly launches a full-scale nuclear attack against the United States. Every major city has become a target of annihilation from an enemy that knows no mercy. America retaliates with what weapons she can launch from her fleet

of nuclear submarines, and both nations smolder in utter ruin. The results of such devastating weapons are catastrophic all over the world. Most of the northern hemisphere is shrouded in unbelievable darkness as smoke and radioactive fallout fill the skies and circle the earth.

The effects of nuclear winter are worse than anyone had ever imagined. Oceans writhe under the trauma of nuclear blasts, and tsunamis are too numerous to count. The loss of life is beyond comprehension.

EVACUATION!
In the midst of all the confusion, born-again Christians have suddenly disappeared, or so it is rumored. Actually, there has been such death and destruction that no one can be sure just what happened to them and, quite frankly, few people even care. The world is in such turmoil that it is now the survival of the fittest.

Roving bands of desperate people seek food and water, and anarchy reigns all over the world. The survivors of the nuclear holocaust are the real victims.

The small contingency of Russian invading forces that survived the slaughter east of Jerusalem have no supply lines from their homeland and no place to retreat. They were part of an invasion that suddenly went strangely wrong as their comrades began killing one another. Now they are abandoned in a desert land that they despise and have no place to hide.

HERE COMES A "KING"
Suddenly a charismatic leader from Europe intervenes in

defense of the Jewish people. He gains an easy military victory over the remaining Russian army that has lost its will to fight. This "champion of the Jewish people" is hailed as the savior of Israel. Some even declare him to be the long-awaited messiah.

Having grasped control of the rest of the world, this leader who has amazing powers of persuasion, confirms a peace treaty with the leaders of Israel and grants them full control over the city of Jerusalem. With great joy and celebration the Jews begin to rebuild their Temple on Temple Mount where Solomon's Temple and the Dome of the Rock once stood. The Jewish priesthood is ready to re-establish their ancient sacrificial rites.

Despite the terrible bloodshed east of the Jordan and the loss of two huge and powerful nations, civil order begins to return to society. The nations rejoice under the deceptive leadership of a one-world government that guarantees peace at last.

ONE HUNDRED FORTY-FOUR THOUSAND YOUNG PEOPLE WITH GOOD NEWS

A strange new sect has suddenly emerged out of all the confusion. One hundred forty-four thousand young Hebrews are suddenly preaching everywhere that Jesus Christ was, in fact, the True Messiah. Multitudes of people from all over the earth are being converted to this fast-growing group.

Two spiritual leaders in Jerusalem claim to be the resurrected Moses and Elijah. They boldly rebuke the world of sin, perversion and unbelief. The religious leaders of

Israel are confronted for their rejection of the Lord Jesus Christ.

TROUBLE IN THE KINGDOM

World peace is short-lived as anarchy begins to rule. In the aftermath of the nuclear holocausts, hunger and human suffering are rampant. Terrorism is worldwide. In an effort to regain control, the new world leader introduces a new international identification system that is implanted in the right hands or foreheads of all true citizens of the New World Order.

The new Temple in Jerusalem is quickly completed, and ancient sacrificial rites are once again begun despite the fact that God's Shekinah Glory is not present above the Mercy Seat as in days of old. Jews from all over the world are now pouring into the land of Israel. Excitement about the prospects of a lasting peace fills the air.

THE ABOMINATION THAT MAKES ALL THINGS DESOLATE

To the shock of Israel's religious leaders, the World Emperor who has been so kind to the Jewish people, and even helped them in the rebuilding of the Temple, has a sudden change of heart. He has entered the Temple and defiled the most Holy Place and declared himself to be God. Everyone on earth is commanded to worship him.

The flow of blood has just begun as Jews, converts to the new Messianic religion, and others in opposition to the New World Order are put to death.

FLEE!

Countless thousands of Jews run in panic from their beloved city and country. Many are hiding in the deserts and canyons of the Judean wilderness. Some have even gone to the ancient ruins of Petra where they are somehow protected and provided with daily food and water.

KING OF KINGS AND LORD OF LORDS!

Then it happens. The whole world looks up into the sky and sees a bright shining light. It looks like a meteor descending upon the earth. Scientists and military leaders claim this strange "satellite" is more than 1500 miles in diameter and it is shaped as a perfect square. Its light is so bright that people everywhere in the world can see it day and night.

Every attempt to destroy this new "threat to mankind" is strangely diverted. The Messianic believers claim that it is the *"sign of the Son of God"* and that Christ is returning to earth to seize control of all governments and power.

The response from the world is immediate. While millions hide in terror, armies begin gathering in the huge valley of Megiddo just north of Jerusalem. The world and its armed forces have come together in unity to do battle against the One Who is coming in a full display of Power and Glory.

YOU KNOW THE REST OF THE STORY

The true Messiah, Jesus, destroys the massive armies of the world at the Battle of Armageddon in righteous conquest and total victory. He then descends upon the Mount of Olives and enters the ancient city of Jerusalem through the Eastern Gate just as the prophets had predicted.

His enemies have been silenced, and the world falls at His feet as He is proclaimed King of kings and Lord of lords!

But His work on earth has just begun. Here is something few people realize.

MIRACLE IN THE DESERT

When Jesus comes down upon the Mount of Olives it shall split to the north and south. Waters shall begin coming out from under the city of Jerusalem, and they will flow to the east and down into the Dead Sea. Waters will also flow to the west and into the Mediterranean Sea. According to *Ezekiel chapter 47*, those *"living waters"* form a river over a mile wide!

The desert is about to be transformed as Scripture promised.

"Then said he unto me, These waters issue out toward the east country, and go down into the Arabah, and go into the sea, and, being brought forth into the sea, the waters shall be healed.

"And it shall come to pass that everything that liveth, which moveth, wherever the rivers shall come, shall live; and there shall be a very great multitude of fish, because these waters shall come there; for they shall be healed; and every thing shall live where the river cometh.

"And it shall come to pass that the fishers shall stand upon it; from Engedi even unto Eneglaim shall be a place to spread forth nets; their fish shall be according to their kinds, as the fish of the Great Sea, exceedingly

many." Ezekiel 47:8-10

The waters of the Dead Sea will be healed. The curse that fell upon Sodom and Gomorrah shall be lifted. The Bible even teaches that the desert lands will blossom – *"The wilderness and the solitary places shall be glad for them; and the desert shall rejoice, and blossom like the rose." Isaiah 35:1*

Today, the hard-working people of Israel are making remarkable and wonderful strides in replanting their land with trees and crops. But when the Lord Jesus Christ comes and sends water into the wastelands, the entire area will once again become like the Garden of Eden!

When I first saw the Dead Sea and knew of this coming transformation that will take place at the hand of the King of kings, all I could say was – "Wow! How incredible! And I am going to be there! Praise God!"

How wonderful and glorious will be the land when Jesus returns and His Kingdom will stretch out across the whole earth. The New Jerusalem orbiting above the ancient city of Jerusalem provides light to a darkened world.

WATERS OF LIFE!
The future miracle of Jesus' coming and sending forth

waters from Jerusalem are beyond the ability of our comprehension. He will make a garden of the wastelands. He will establish His long-awaited kingdom on earth. Then, and only then, will the people *"beat their weapons into plows."*

There will be no more terrorism and bloodshed as the Lord establishes His Millennial Kingdom on earth!

Those "living waters" are a beautiful picture of what happens in the lives of people when they encounter the saving grace of the Lord Jesus Christ. Lives that were once like a desert place are transformed. Lives that were once wasted and barren become fruitful.

Jesus spoke of this miraculous transformation of the human spirit when he cried out –

> *"In that day, that great day of the feast, Jesus stood and cried out, saying, If any man thirst, let him come unto Me, and drink. He that believeth on Me, as the scripture hath said, out of his heart shall flow <u>rivers of living water</u>. But this spoke He of the Spirit, whom they that believe on Him should receive; for the Holy Spirit was not yet given because Jesus was not yet glorified." John 7:37-39*

Recipients of God's grace and mercy become the dwelling place of God the Holy Spirit. Like a river of living water, He brings life and beauty to all that He touches.

If your life is like a desert wilderness, can I encourage you to place your faith in the Lord Jesus Christ?

He alone can satisfy every longing in your heart and life.

He alone can offer you the gift of eternal life.

He alone can give you real and eternal hope in a world that is quickly falling apart and will soon destroy itself, as we have discovered in this study.

RUN TO HIM FOR SAFETY!

I would be remiss if I did not give you clear biblical instructions about how to receive the Lord Jesus Christ as Savior and Lord. Read each of these verses very carefully. Ask God to reveal His truth to your heart.

BAD NEWS

"For all have sinned and come short of the glory of God." Romans 3:23

"As it is written, There is none righteous, no not one: There is none that understandeth, there is none that seeketh after God." Romans 3:10-11

"But your sins have separated between you and your God, and your sins have hidden His face from you, that He will not hear." Isaiah 59:2

"The soul that sinneth, it shall die." Ezekiel 18:4

"For the wages of sin is death . . ." Romans 6:23

GOOD NEWS!

"For the wages of sin is death, <u>but the gift of God is</u>

eternal life through Jesus Christ our Lord." *Romans 6:23*

"*All we like sheep have gone astray; we have turned every one to his own way, and the LORD has laid on Him the iniquity of us all.*" *Isaiah 53:6*

"*That if thou shalt confess with thy mouth the Lord Jesus, and shalt believe in thine heart that God hath raised Him for the dead, thou shalt be saved. For with the heart man believeth unto righteousness; and with the mouth confession is made unto salvation.*" *Romans 10:9-10*

IT HAPPENED TO ME AND IT CAN HAPPEN TO YOU

I grew up in a home that didn't know the love and grace of the Lord Jesus Christ. We weren't opposed to the things of God; we just didn't know anything about Christ or of His offer of salvation.

As a child, I spent several years on the family ranch near Durango, Colorado. Things weren't pleasant at home in western Michigan because our dad had a problem with drinking. My aunt and uncle were more than glad to have a youngster around because they had no children of their own.

Those were wonderful days living out in the Rocky Mountain wilderness with no electricity nor running water. My love for the Colorado Rockies has never diminished since those years on the ranch and I am grateful to still be living near the mountains.

Leaning Chimney Ranch near Durango, Colorado

I remember praying as a child that my family would somehow stay together and find happiness. When my aunt came out to where I was playing one afternoon, she had a letter in her hand from my mother back home. Things were not good at home, and it was decided that I should spend another school year at the ranch instead of returning home as planned. I had pretty mixed emotions – I was glad to stay out west on the ranch, but I was also angry at God for not answering my prayers for my family. I wondered what kind of God wouldn't even hear the prayers of a little boy for his family.

I remember cursing and throwing toys up into the air as if I could somehow hit God and maybe hurt His feelings. I told Him that I never wanted anything to do with Him again and to just leave me alone.

David, Chuck, and Phil Anderson on the ranch in 1950. By God's grace, we all came to a knowledge of the Lord Jesus Christ!

I'm so glad that there are some prayers that He does not answer!

Several years later, my oldest brother Phil became a believer while he was overseas in the Marine Corps. I thought the idol of my life had somehow lost his mind.

Then, my other brother David, Phil's twin, also accepted Christ as Savior and Lord. It wasn't long before my mother followed suit and also received Him as Savior. She was 55 years old when she made that life-changing decision.

After returning to Michigan as a teenager, I spent several years in Detroit with my dad and grandmother. I wanted nothing to do with that Christian stuff. But then my best friend and his mother and sister all became believers in Jesus. I felt surrounded, but I wasn't ready to surrender.

It was agreed that I would spend the last two years of high school living with my mother in the little village of Lamont. I went from the huge Redford High School to the little Coopersville High School fourteen miles west of Grand Rapids.

Friends I had known in grade school invited me to a series of teen meetings called YouthArama at the Civic Auditorium in Grand Rapids. For the first time I realized that Jesus Christ was God in the flesh, and that He had come to this world to save sinners.

There was no doubt about my being a sinner – after all, I had cursed at God and told Him that I hated Him.

On my sixteenth birthday, I responded to God's prompting in my heart to receive the Lord Jesus Christ as Savior. My, what a wonderful change began to occur as I had an immediate hunger for the Bible.

Just before joining the United States Marine Corps in 1961, our dad deserted the family and ran off with a younger woman he had met in a bar. We didn't see him for nearly eight years.

I had given up on Dad and didn't think that anything could ever change him, but my mother faithfully prayed for his salvation year after year even though she had been abandoned.

Little did I know when I attended the Billy Graham Crusade meetings in Los Angeles in 1963, that my dad was in that huge crowd! Years later, as his "friend" was dying of cirrhosis of the liver, a pastor walked into their hospital room looking for another family. He graciously spoke to them and shared the gospel. Both of them acknowledged their need of a Savior and received the Lord Jesus Christ!

By then, I had gotten out of the Marine Corps and completed Bible School in Grand Rapids, where I met my wife, JoEllen. She and I moved to Colorado to do a church-planting ministry and were living in Colorado Springs.

To my amazement, we got a telephone call from my dad one day. Soon he came for a visit. What a joy to have a dad who was now a fellow-believer in the Lord Jesus Christ!

He went back to visit the rest of the family in Grand Rapids. My mother soon retired from nursing and joined him in California until he retired. They spent the rest of their days together. What an incredible thing God can do in each of our lives if we will just believe in Him and surrender our pride and wills to Him!

Knowing the Lord Jesus Christ and experiencing forgiveness for our many sins is very real and wonderful. He wants you to believe and be spiritually born into His eternal family.

GOT QUESTIONS?
God bless you and help you to come to a personal knowledge of His Son, the Lord Jesus Christ! If you have questions, please don't hesitate to contact me. I will personally respond to any questions you may have.

We have established a web site so that persons with questions can get answers in the privacy of their own homes. Please don't hesitate to contact us through **http://DiscoveryNews.us/** or **DiscoveryNews1@aol.com**

Chuck and JoEllen Anderson at the Sea of Galilee
November 2005

Printed in the United States
81280LV00003B/148-501